Praise for *Gramm*

"A five-star grammar guide written by a superb editor. Spare yourself a lifetime of grammatical grief: Buy this book!"
— **James Randall Miller, author of *Untangling Claire* and *Howling Across Bridges***

"I wish I'd had this book when I began my career as a professor; I would have made it required reading for my graduate students! While most were excellent scientists, writing did not come easily to them. Buy this easy-to-understand guide: It will be invaluable to you and any student who struggles with English grammar."
— **Rajan Suri, Industrial Engineering Professor Emeritus, international speaker, author, educator**

"Whether in person or on the phone, whether by text, email or online chat, my staff members must present themselves as financial experts. Our writing and speaking shape our bank's image and support our brand. Kathy's Killer Tips — easy, quick and fun to read — keep us on our toes and inspire customer confidence."
— **Jude Lengell, VP and Manager of Deposit Operations and Customer Support**

"Email dominates communication in the business world. Your messages make an immediate and indelible impression. Keep these Killer Tips at your fingertips and consult them often to help convey that you're an intelligent, well-educated, conscientious business professional."
— **Scott Fredrick, CEO, Phoenix Products Company Inc.**

"As a publicity expert and professional writer who cranks out content by the barrel, I appreciate Kathy's wisdom and candor. You will too. Whether you're writing a book, selling freelance articles, sharing content online or applying for a job, buy this book and keep it handy. It can keep you out of trouble and make you a whole lot smarter."
— **Joan Stewart, PublicityHound.com**

"The Ruthless Editor's Grammar for People Who Hate Rules *is designed to instruct, explain and encourage the reader with a series of easy-to-follow lessons. I highly recommend this informative book!"*
— **Kathleen M. Galvin, Professor, Communication Studies, Northwestern University**

"My reports for attorneys, judges and healthcare professionals have to be clear and concise. I count on Kathy's Killer Tips to answer any questions I have about word and punctuation use."
— **Cynthia Walters, Forensic Mental Health Counselor**

"Because 95% or more of my daily communication is by email, clear, concise writing is critically important. Misunderstandings can be costly in terms of both money and relationships. I keep Kathy's Killer Tips close at hand."
— **Dan Swanson, Vice President Preconstruction, JP Cullen & Sons Inc.**

"In the first 30 seconds of meeting, a prospective client will decide whether or not you are credible, competent and trustworthy. When first encounters are electronic documents, your success relies on vocabulary, punctuation and grammar. This easy-to-follow guide will ensure that you get to the next step."
— **Jacqui Sakowski, International Sales Coach, consultant, author**

"Kathy uses relevant examples to guide us in using proper grammar. A reliable resource for general as well as technical and scientific writing, this practical book is perfect for both native and non-native English writers and speakers."
— **Dawn Wagenknecht, Clinical Laboratory Manager, Ph.D. candidate**

"I'm a Ruthless Editor fan and regularly follow her blog. The Killer Tips in this book force me to re-examine my own writing, reminding me of what I know and teaching me things I need to know."
— **Charles Myhill, old-school journalist, world traveler**

"Engineers in every field have to write clearly; career progression depends on being able to capably articulate complex technical issues and ideas. I consult Grammar for People Who Hate Rules *often, and I highly recommend it to others in my field."*
— **Andrew Sprouse, Software Engineer**

"Not a day goes by that I don't question my punctuation or word use in email correspondence with clients, customers, business associates and friends. Kathy's book stays right next to my computer!" — **Georgia Janisch, Dietitian**

"I almost lost a prestigious national award by submitting presentation material with several grammatical errors. Kathleen's book will always be on my desk."
— **David Young, owner Studio Four Magazine, author of *The Other Side of Luck,* retired university faculty**

GRAMMAR

FOR PEOPLE WHO HATE RULES

GRAMMAR

FOR PEOPLE WHO HATE RULES

Killer Tips From The Ruthless Editor

KATHLEEN A. WATSON

Contact the author for quantity pricing of 10 or more books.

Address inquires to the author via:
email: Kathy@RuthlessEditor.com
website: www.RuthlessEditor.com

Printed in the United States of America
Ruthless Editor Press
Author photo by Carolyn Alane Tretina

ISBN-13: 978-0-9976646-0-7 (paperback)
ISBN-13: 978-0-9976646-1-4 (ebook)

For Althea, my extraordinary mother

Good English, well spoken and well written,
will open more doors than a college degree.
Bad English will slam doors
you didn't even know existed.

— William Raspberry

CONTENTS

3 BONUS TIPS

APPENDIX

Quizzes

WELCOME

Do you dread writing a report or class assignment? Worry that your email to your CEO might have embarrassing mistakes? Panic when you find out you have to speak at a meeting and agonize that you'll use a wrong word?

If so, you're in the right place.

The tips in this book, a straightforward guide to many of today's common word and punctuation errors, can help you make the right choices. It's not meant to be an explanation of every grammar puzzle, and you won't find terms such as *subordinating conjunction for the dependent clause.*

What you will find are short, easy-to-follow tips and examples about which word to choose, when to insert a comma, what to capitalize — and more.

Our digital-age shortcuts don't foster elegant prose. My Killer Tips will remind you how today's Standard English should look and sound, modeling the way educated people use language.

You're judged by the way you write and speak. Whether you're a student, a business professional, an author, a blogger, a professional speaker, or someone who simply wants to fine-tune your communication skills, this book is for you.

- ✓ **Killer Tip:** Before you dig in, check page 132 to refresh your memory on some basic parts of speech discussed throughout the book.

INTRODUCTION

Confused by Grammar? You're Not Alone!
Many claim that English is one of the most confusing
languages in the world. We have words that sound the
same but are spelled differently and have different
meanings: there, their and they're, for example, or to,
too and two.

Add to that an abundance of words that are spelled the
same but pronounced differently: I'll read that book today,
but I read a different one yesterday, and The wind blows
as I wind the clock.

Of all the world's languages, English has one of the largest
vocabularies; there are lots of words to learn!

Grammar helps us structure our sometimes-convoluted
language so others can understand us. It encompasses the
words we choose and how we punctuate them, indicating
when to pause or stop, when to raise our voice or show
emotion, when we're asking a question versus making
a statement.

Many consider grammar confusing, hard to master and
downright boring. In today's world of abbreviated digital
communication, others consider grammar irrelevant.

Why Does Grammar Still Matter?
Productive personal and business relationships require
clear communication. Writing and speaking well gives you
an advantage. Mastering the grammar of Standard English
can determine whether you get into the college of your
choice, land the job of your dreams, or get the promotion
you've worked so hard for.

I prefer to talk of grammar in terms of guidelines rather than rules. Language evolves and rules can change or vary, depending on the style guide or "expert." Yet our need to be understood endures.

Although Standard English has few absolutes, there are preferred ways of stringing words together. That's why you need this book: I want to help you write — and speak — in a way that reflects today's conventional usage. I want your language to open doors.

Grammar Doesn't Have to be Hard

I believe examples are the best way to master grammar, and I'm not alone. Research conducted at the University of Arizona reviewed 250 studies about how to teach writing to students in grades 3–7. It revealed that neither traditional grammar instruction such as diagramming sentences nor teaching rules of grammar is effective.

American author Joan Didion agrees: "Grammar is a piano I play by ear."

Learning grammar parallels learning to play music by ear. If we read and hear what is considered Standard English — or better yet, truly eloquent writing and speaking — we can master it by osmosis. We can learn what "sounds right" without memorizing arcane rules.

Whether you need an introduction to English grammar or a reminder of all you've forgotten, make this book your reliable companion.

Note: Many usage recommendations in this book follow The Associated Press Stylebook, a resource used widely by journalists, students, editors and writers in all professions.

WORDS

USE and MISUSE

The digital age does not foster eloquence.

— Lucy Silver

1

Active vs. Passive Voice: Keep Your Writing Lively and Readable

Active voice is more lively and easier to read. It makes clear *who* has done — or should do — something. It prevents wordy, convoluted sentences.

In active voice, the subject of the sentence clearly is the *doer* of the action. In passive voice, the doer of the action is identified in an indirect way.

active: I am holding the baby.
passive: The baby is being held by me.

active: Rob tromped on the gas as his car sped away.
passive: The gas was tromped on by Rob as his car sped away.

active: Jim is considering what action to take.
passive: What action to take is being considered by Jim.

Passive voice isn't always wrong. It's used appropriately in scientific writing, which should sound objective and where the action is more important than who does it, and in crime reports, when authorities don't know the doer.

Scientific passive:

▶ The subjects of the study were interviewed by each interviewer.

▶ The results have been replicated by a new group of researchers.

Crime report passive:

▶ The branch bank was robbed sometime between 3 and 4:40 a.m.

▶ The woman was stabbed as she approached her car.

Note the presence of some form of the verb *to be* in all passive examples *(is, am, are, was, were, have/has been)*:
... baby *is being* held ... gas pedal *was tromped* on ... action *is being* considered ... subjects *were* interviewed by ... results *have been* replicated ... branch bank *was* robbed ... woman *was* stabbed ...

Government documents can get wordy, and passive voice sometimes is the culprit.

passive: The following information must be included in the application for it to be considered complete.
active: You must include the following information in your application.

passive: Regulations have been proposed by the EPA.
active: The EPA has proposed regulations.

✓ **Killer Tip:** Convert the twisted, dull-sounding construction of passive voice to active by using a subject-verb-object sequence and avoiding forms of the verb *to be*.

2

Your English Teacher Was Wrong: You *May* Start a Sentence With *And, But, So*

Should you start a sentence with *And?* What about *But* or *So?*

It depends.

And, but and *so* serve as conjunctions; they're joiners. They can be the perfect transition between one thought and another when your writing has an informal tone.

Here are examples that use these informal joiners:
▶ Beth grabbed the bucket of water, set out on a dead run and reached the gate just as it was swinging shut. *And* she didn't spill a drop!
▶ Aaron promised he would never take his parents' car without permission. *But* can you guess what he did last night?
▶ The longer thumb-sucking continues, the higher the likelihood your child will need orthodontic treatment. *So* when should you intervene, and what should you do?

Here are the same examples with more-formal joiners — a conjunction and two prepositions:

► Beth grabbed the bucket of water, set out on a dead run and reached the gate just as it was swinging shut. *However*, she didn't spill a drop!

► Aaron promised he would never take his parents' car without permission. *Despite* that pledge, can you guess what he did last night?

► The longer thumb-sucking continues, the higher the likelihood your child will need orthodontic treatment. *Given* the potential for that undesirable outcome, when should you intervene, and what should you do?

Good writers use the fewest and the shortest words. Good writers also consider their audience.

If you're writing a dissertation, a thesis, a report on research findings or any treatise, you'll be wise to use conjunctions such as these to convey a formal tone: *however, nevertheless, moreover, furthermore, additionally*.

But if you're writing informally, there are many cases where *And, But* and *So* — all a single syllable — are acceptable ways to start a sentence.

✓ **Killer Quote:** "There is a widespread belief — one with no historical or grammatical foundation — that it is an error to begin a sentence with a conjunction such as and, but or so. In fact, a substantial percentage (often as many as 10 percent) of the sentences in first-rate writing begin with conjunctions. It has been so for centuries, and even the most conservative grammarians have followed this practice."

— The Chicago Manual of Style

3

Don't Leave *As far as* Hanging: Anchor It With a Verb

Lots of today's communication is abbreviated, but here's usage I hear daily that is so shortened, it's grammatically incorrect:

▶ As far as dogs, collies are my favorite.
▶ As far as weather, we're expecting a great weekend.
▶ As far as movies, I'd rather watch them in a theater than at home.
▶ As far as a house, we're looking for a two-story.

***As far as* is a prepositional phrase; it requires something further — a verb in these examples — to help it make sense:**

▶ As far as dogs *go*, collies are my favorite.
▶ As far as weather *is concerned*, we're expecting a great weekend.
▶ As far as movies *are concerned*, I'd rather watch them in a theater than at home.
▶ As far as our house choices *go*, we're looking for a two-story.

You also could correct the first set of examples by substituting the prepositional phrase *with regard to:*

- ▶ With regard to dogs, collies are my favorite.
- ▶ With regard to weather, we're expecting a great weekend.

Or you could use *in terms of:*
- ▶ In terms of movies, I'd rather watch them in a theater than at home.
- ▶ In terms of house styles, we're looking for a two-story.

- ✓ **Killer Tip:** Don't cut *as far as* or similar prepositional phrases to a point that leaves your statement grammatically incomplete. *As far as grammar is concerned,* you'll sound better educated if you include an appropriate verb form that links this common prepositional phrase to the rest of your sentence.

4

You Had Better Read This!

We know that language is constantly evolving, but sometimes that evolution creates either improper word use or confusion — or both.

I'd been hearing and reading something that struck me as wrong, but I had to stop and think — and do some research — to determine where the problem was.

And as is so often the case, examples explain preferred usage better than long, complicated rules.

What's wrong with these statements?
- ▶ The candidates better decide soon if they're going to run.
- ▶ You better not be late for the meeting.
- ▶ We better go before it starts to rain.

When you are making a recommendation or issuing a warning as these statements do, *had better* is the appropriate construction:
- ▶ The candidates had better decide soon if they're going to run.
- ▶ You had better not be late for the meeting.
- ▶ We had better go before it starts to rain.

In speaking, it's often easier to use a contraction:

▶ We'd better go before it starts to rain.
▶ You'd better not be late for the meeting.

✓ **Killer Tip:** If you are stating that someone *should* or *ought* to do something, *had better,* not simply *better,* is the proper way to express it. Note that *had better* can imply that something negative could happen if a person fails to do what is recommended.

5

Cement vs. Concrete and Other C-Words That Confuse

Sometimes context enables clear communication, even when you use the wrong word or combination of words. Yet no one wants to make an obvious mistake because of lack of knowledge or understanding.

Here are three sets of words beginning with c that often are misused.

cement vs. concrete

You don't have to be in construction to refer to *cement* or *concrete* from time to time. However, those who work in the trades are more apt to know that you don't say *cement* sidewalk or *cement* block wall. *Cement* is the powder that, when mixed with water, sand and gravel, hardens to become *concrete*.

▶ The cement pour was delayed because of torrential rains.
▶ He hired someone to paint the concrete blocks that form his basement walls.
▶ Tree roots have created cracks in my concrete sidewalk.

continuous vs. continual

Continuous refers to something that goes on nonstop, without interruption. *Continual* implies repetition with intervals or breaks in the action.

▶ The continuous hum of the fluorescent light distracted her.

▶ In many regions, continual April showers bring May flowers.

compared to vs. compared with

There is little difference between *compared to* and *compared with*, but in general, *compared to* more often implies that two things are similar or belong in the same category.

▶ She compared her own soufflé to one she had tasted while traveling in France.

▶ He compared the slowly recovering economy to a wobbly newborn calf struggling to stand.

When you want to emphasize differences, *compared with* is preferred.

▶ Our business plan, when compared with theirs, includes much more detail.

▶ Compared with my MacBook Pro, my first computer was a dinosaur.

✓ **Killer Tip:** *Cement* of course can be a verb as well: Let's get some glue and see if we can *cement* the pieces of this broken pot together.

6

Grammar Stickler Banishes
comprised of From Wikipedia

When I came across an online story headlined "One Man's Quest to Rid Wikipedia of Exactly One Grammatical Mistake," I of course had to find out who this fellow grammar stickler was and which error had become his obsession.

A software engineer writing as Giraffedata, this stickler edits Wikipedia reports for the incorrect use of *comprise*. *He* claims to have made 47,000 corrections since 2007.

I'd had *comprise* vs. *compose* on my list of potential topics for years, but so many people use *comprised of* incorrectly that I'd considered it a lost cause.

Here are examples of *comprise* as well as words with similar meanings.

Comprise means to contain, to include, to consist of:
- ▶ Congress comprises 435 representatives.
- ▶ His car collection comprises eight Model T Fords.
- ▶ The committee comprises six women and eight men.

Compose **means to form in combination, to make up, to constitute:**

▶ Congress is composed of 435 representatives.
▶ His car collection is composed of eight Model T Fords.
▶ The committee is composed of six women and eight men.

Consist **means to be formed of or made up of:**

▶ Congress consists of 435 representatives.
▶ His car collection consists of eight Model T Fords.
▶ The committee consists of six women and eight men.

Constitute **means to make up, to be components of or to be elements of:**

▶ Four hundred thirty-five representatives constitute Congress.
▶ Eight Model T Fords constitute his car collection.
▶ Six women and eight men constitute the committee.

When you use *comprise*, you first mention *the whole* of something and follow with its components:

▶ Congress ... 435 representatives
▶ car collection ... eight Model T Fords
▶ committee ... six women, eight men

When you use *constitute*, you first mention *the components* of something and follow with the whole:

▶ 435 representatives ... Congress
▶ eight Model T Fords ... car collection
▶ six women and eight men ... committee

✓ **Killer Tip:** Something can be *composed of* or can *consist of* elements, but it can't be *comprised of* or *constituted of* elements.

7

Concerning and Disconcerting: Similar Sound, Different Meanings

Concerning means relating to something or someone; regarding; about. It's a preposition, and it most often is used to introduce something. It is followed by words that complete a thought.

Here are examples of how *concerning* is used correctly:

▶ We met with the traffic director concerning adding a stop sign at the school crosswalk.

▶ Seth and I had a conversation concerning the new supermarket being built in our community.

▶ The manager's weak approach to dealing with issues concerning habitually late employees is unacceptable.

Note that *related to*, *regarding* or *about* could easily be substituted for *concerning* in each case.

Here are incorrect ways to use *concerning* that seem to be popping up in conversations, in news reports and in public commentary:

- ▶ Facebook has some concerning content.
- ▶ It's concerning that so few students follow the dress code.
- ▶ There have been a number of failures in the inspection process that I find concerning.

People are beginning to use *concerning* to mean that something is cause for concern, worrisome, alarming or troublesome. However, that usage is not Standard English. **Disconcerting** is one correct way to express concern.

These rewrites for the three examples above correctly express something worrisome, something troubling, something that is causing concern:
- ▶ Some content on Facebook is disconcerting.
- ▶ Some content on Facebook concerns me.

- ▶ It's disconcerting that so many students don't follow the dress code.
- ▶ It's troublesome that so few students follow the dress code.

- ▶ There have been failures in the inspection process that I find worrisome.
- ▶ Failures in the inspection process are of concern to me.

You can say, "I find his behavior concerning," and hope others interpret your statement to mean that you have concerns about someone's behavior.

But careful speakers and writers might respond with the query, "His behavior concerning what?"

- ✓ **Killer Tip:** Avoid ambiguity. Promote clarity. Recognize the difference between *concerning*, which means related to, and *disconcerting*, which means something unsettling.

8

Dangling Modifiers:
Confusing to Downright Silly

I know, I know ... I've heard all the jokes about dangling modifiers. But when it comes to grammar, they are no laughing matter.

A dangling modifier is a phrase that either is in the wrong place or modifies the wrong thing. These misplaced or poorly worded phrases can create confusion, or they can totally change the meaning of what you intend to say.

Or they can sound darned silly.

Having finished eating dinner, the dishes were loaded into the dishwasher.
problem: The dishes did not eat dinner; people ate dinner.
better: Having finished eating dinner, we loaded the dishes into the dishwasher.

Without knowing her phone number, it was impossible to contact her.
problem: Who didn't know her number? It?
better: Without knowing her phone number, I found it impossible to contact her.

At age 7, Josh's father entered the Army.
problem: No one's father could enter the Army at age 7.
better: When Josh was 7, his father entered the Army.

Buried in an old cedar chest, Kia found her cheerleading sweater.
problem: Kia wasn't buried in the old cedar chest, her sweater was.
better: Buried in an old cedar chest was the cheerleading sweater Kia had worn.
better yet: Kia found her cheerleading sweater buried in an old cedar chest.

Walking home last night, the porch light was visible a block away.
problem: The porch light was not walking home last night.
better: As I walked home last night, I saw the porch light from a block away.

To avoid dangling modifiers, pay attention to the order of your words and to the *doer* of the action.

✓ **Killer Quote:** "Miscommunication lies at the heart of most unhappy situations." — George Davies

9

Drunk, Snuck, Healthful: Usage Tips for the Pickiest Grammarians

Which is it: drank or drunk, sneaked or snuck, healthy or healthful?

Forms of these words seem to cause confusion, which is why so many people often choose the wrong one from a grammatical perspective.

Using one over the other doesn't necessarily contribute to misunderstanding, but if you're particular about language, heed these examples:

drank / drunk

► I drink orange juice daily.
► He drank a glass of lemonade yesterday.
► She had drunk five cups of coffee by noon.

I often hear *had drank*, which is incorrect. My theory is that we associate *drunk* with someone who abuses alcohol, giving it negative connotations. We avoid saying *had drunk* because we don't like the way it sounds.

sneak / snuck

▶ He intends to sneak out of today's meeting.

▶ He sneaked out yesterday as well.

▶ He has sneaked out every time a meeting has lasted more than two hours.

No one will misunderstand if you say, "He snuck out yesterday," or "He has snuck out of many meetings." But *sneaked* is still considered Standard English and is preferred by many respected sources.

healthy / healthful

Healthy describes someone or something that enjoys good health:

▶ Rover's energy and antics confirm he's a healthy puppy.

▶ Healthy populations of earthworms help gardens grow.

▶ If you want to be healthy, you should eat right and get enough sleep.

Healthful describes something that will create good health:

▶ A healthful diet includes lots of fresh fruits and vegetables.

▶ She maintained a healthful routine of swimming and lifting weights.

▶ Poor air quality does not make for a healthful working environment.

✓ **Killer Tip:** Language evolves. *Healthful* and *healthy* are gradually being accepted by many as interchangeable. In a few more years, will we find even top grammar guides approving *have drank* and *snuck?* I'll wait for broad consensus before I accept those forms in my writing and editing.

10

Fact vs. Factoid: Don't Confuse the Two

Word meanings and their usage evolve and change. However, here's one I've been keeping my eye on for years: *factoid*.

I first heard the word in graduate school, assuming it meant a tiny fact. I was wrong.

New York Times columnist Gail Collins let loose with *factoid* in her Jan. 2, 2015, column. She wrote:

> When Hillary Clinton thinks about running for president, do you think she contemplates the fact that no Democrat has been elected to succeed another Democrat since James Buchanan in 1856? We bring you this factoid in honor of the beginning of the 2016 election season.

Collins obviously chose *factoid* to convey an accepted historical fact. But consider the term's history. American writer Norman Mailer coined it in his 1973 biography of Marilyn Monroe.

Mailer described a factoid as "facts which have no existence before appearing in a magazine or newspaper." He created the word by combining *fact* with *oid*, meaning similar but not the same.

The Washington Times described Mailer's new word as referring to "something that looks like a fact, could be a fact, but in fact is not a fact."

Bottom line: A factoid is something that appears to be a fact but is not accurate or verified.

Other sources define factoid this way:
▶ purporting to be factual or a phony statistic
▶ seeming to be though not necessarily factual
▶ a piece of unverified or inaccurate information that is presented in the press as factual, often as part of a publicity effort, and that is then accepted as true because of frequent repetition

Here's the problem:
Some sources define factoid as a little-known bit of true information; trivial but interesting data; a brief, somewhat interesting fact.

Something either is or is not a fact. A word with two opposite, contradictory meanings at the least misleads readers, and at the worst misinforms readers. I intend to stick to the original meaning of *factoid* as Mailer crafted it.

✓ **Killer Tip:** Unless you are certain your reading audience understands the difference between *fact* and *factoid*, avoid using *factoid*.

11

What Do You Say: Lie or Lay?

Are you among many people who still get confused about lie versus lay? You're not alone!

Here are sample sentences and tips on how to remember when to use *lie* and when to use *lay*.

lie: to recline
- ▶ Grandpa likes to *lie* on the couch every day for a nap.
- ▶ Nicole can't wait to *lie* on the beach in Florida.
- ▶ Steve thinks he should *lie* on several mattresses before deciding which one to buy.

Tip: *Lie* shares three letters — *l, i* and *e* — and a similar *i* sound with *recline*.

Here are other verb forms of *lie*:
- ▶ Grandpa *is lying* on the couch now.
- ▶ He *will lie* on the couch tomorrow.
- ▶ Grandpa *lay* on the couch yesterday.*
- ▶ He *has lain* on the couch every day for a month.
- ▶ He *would have lain* there sooner if he'd had the chance.

Try to remember: lie, lay, has lain
You want to recline, to *lie*, on something soft. The letter *d* is a hard sound, so *laid* should not be used when talking about reclining.

lay: to place
▶ Grandpa asked me to *lay* his glasses on the nightstand.
▶ Nicole wants me to *lay* her towel on the sand.
▶ The mattress salesperson told Steve to *lay* his shoes on the floor.

Tip: *Lay* shares two letters — *l* and *a* — and a similar *a* sound with *place*.

Here are other verb forms of *lay:*
▶ Grandpa left his glasses *lying* on the nightstand.*
▶ I *will lay* Grandpa's glasses on the nightstand tomorrow.
▶ I *laid* them on the nightstand without being asked.
▶ He often *has laid* them there himself.
▶ I would not *have laid* them there if he hadn't asked.

Avoid *layed* in all cases; it is nonstandard English.

* You probably noticed two exceptions. I confess that I have yet to find a catchy, easy way to remember them:

▶ The past tense of *lie* is *lay*, the verb that also means to place: *Lie* down, and then *lay* your glasses on the table.
▶ Although you lay objects on something, once they get there, they are described as lying: *Lay* your glasses on the table and hope they still are *lying* there when you wake up.

✓ **Killer Tip:** *Lie* is to recline. *Lay* is to place. There are two confusing exceptions: 1. The past tense of lie is *lay*. 2. An object that is placed somewhere is *lying* there.

12

What Was John Wayne's Maiden Name?

Legendary for his rugged masculinity, actor John Wayne was born Marion Robert Morrison. Can you imagine a reporter interviewing him and asking him what his *maiden name* was?

Consider Miriam-Webster's definition of maiden name:
a woman's family name before she is married

According to dictionary.com, maiden name is:
a woman's surname before her marriage

Do those definitions not smack of the assumption — or at least the implication — that all women eventually marry?

We're in the 21st century. There are better, more gender-neutral, more inclusive — or simply more accurate — terms: *childhood name*, *original name*, or my preference, *birth name*.

Some sources suggest *family name* or *father's family name*.

Times change, maiden name persists
The outdated descriptor *maiden name* still is used in

everyday conversations, by writers, and on forms both men and women complete for any number of official uses.

Consider this June 2015 headline in *The New York Times:*

Maiden Names, on the Rise Again

The article reports that roughly 20 percent of women retain their birth name after marrying, rather than legally becoming known by their husband's family name. Another 10 percent or so hyphenate their name or legally change it while continuing to use their birth name professionally.

Political correctness and sexism aside, it makes sense to use the more inclusive and gender-neutral term *birth name* when inquiring about or referring to anyone's original name. It can apply to men as well as to women — or to spouses of any union.

If you work in human resources or have forms in your company that request a *maiden name*, I hope you'll encourage those who oversee that department to consider a more inclusive term.

Were he still around, I'll bet John Wayne would concur.

✓ **Killer Quote:** "Talk low, talk slow, and don't say too much." — John Wayne

13

The Dilemma of Me, Myself and I

As children, many of us probably had our moms correct us when we said, "Me and Billy are going for a bike ride."

"Billy and I," she would admonish.

"Can me and Jenny have a lemonade stand?" we may have inquired.

"Jenny and I," Mom would correct.

It's not surprising that so many of us steer clear of *me* in places where it truly is the correct choice.

me vs. I
▶ My boss is taking *Jim and I* to lunch.
▶ My boss is taking *Jim and me* to lunch.

Which is correct? Jim and me.

The quick-and-easy way to make the right choice is to eliminate Jim from the statement. You wouldn't say, "My boss is taking *I* to lunch." You would say, "My boss is taking *me* to lunch." Adding Jim doesn't change anything — except the amount of the bill!

me vs. myself

The same type of example shows how *myself* can be misused. How many times have you seen this phrasing: "Please contact Sarah or myself with questions."

Again, if you eliminated Sarah, you would not say, "Please contact myself with questions." *Me* is the right choice: "Please contact Sarah or *me* with questions."

- ▶ *I* is a subject, the doer of an action.
- ▶ *Me* is an object, the receiver of an action.
- ▶ *Myself* is a reflexive pronoun: "I try not to take myself too seriously." It often is used for emphasis: "I myself would never take a sick day that wasn't warranted."

Mom was right about the courtesy of mentioning another person's name before your own; however, I'm sure she didn't intend for you to structure your sentences with grammatical errors.

✓ **Killer Tip:** When mentioning yourself and another person, consider how the sentence would be phrased without that person's name to determine whether *me*, *myself* or *I* fits.

14

Meandering Modifiers Miscommunicate

Modifiers are supposed to add meaning or clarification. A misplaced modifier can do just the opposite.

Consider the differing connotations of *often*:
▶ College students who meet *often* with their advisers make better career choices.
▶ College students who meet with their advisers *often* make better career choices.

Are we to understand that students have to meet frequently with their advisers to make better career choices? Or should we assume that just one meeting with an adviser is enough to result in better choices?

For clarity, a modifier should be placed closest to the word or phrase it is meant to influence or explain.

Consider the differing connotations of *almost*:
▶ Sam has *almost* failed every exam this semester.
▶ Sam has failed *almost* every exam this semester.

There's a big difference between *almost* — but not quite — failing every exam and failing *almost every* — the majority of — exams.

Consider the differing connotations of *only*:

▶ You *only* can apply for esurance online.
▶ You can apply for esurance *only* online.

The first *only* could modify *you*, conveying that you are the only person who can apply for esurance online. A reader would not likely draw that conclusion, but it's open to interpretation.

Or *only* could modify *can apply*, suggesting that you can apply for esurance online, but you can do nothing else electronically with esurance. In other words, you can't file a claim online, you can't get responses to questions online, and you can't set up online payments.

The second *only* example clearly communicates that online is the only way you can apply for esurance.

Only meanders more than any other modifier. These examples show how modifier placement changes meaning:

▶ *Only* Danny sang at the party. (No one else sang.)
▶ Danny *only* sang at the party. (He didn't dance or play the piano.)
▶ Danny sang *only* at the party. (He didn't sing elsewhere.)

✓ **Killer Tip:** Corral your meandering modifiers. Make sure they end up closest to the word or phrase whose meaning they influence.

15

Confusion About Myriad and Kudos

Myriad and *kudos* are of Greek origin, which could be why people sometimes have a hard time knowing exactly how to use them. When you consider that there is disagreement about usage even in respected sources, you face a dilemma.

myriad: many, a countless or infinite number; also: both numerous and diverse

In the following examples, either *myriad* or *a myriad of* would be acceptable, but I — as do many writers and editors — prefer the first sentence of each set. Good writing expresses a thought in the fewest words.

▶ She provides tech support for a network with *myriad* computers.

▶ She provides tech support for a network with *a myriad of* computers.

▶ The sky glows with *myriad* stars.

▶ The sky glows with *a myriad of* stars.

▶ He read *myriad* articles about nutrition before he started his diet.

▶ He read *a myriad of* articles about nutrition before he started his diet.

kudos: credit or praise for an achievement

The most important thing to remember about kudos, beyond its definition, is that although the *s* makes *kudos* appear to be plural, it is singular. It means *glory* in Greek. You would not say or write: I'm sending you *a kudo (a glory)* for the great job you did on the essay.

▶ Bank staff earned *kudos* for their high customer service rating.

▶ *Kudos* to Mia for winning the tennis championship.

✓ **Killer Tip:** It's doubtful that anyone will summon the grammar police if you use *a myriad of* rather than simply *myriad*, but it's generally better to use the fewest words.

16

Grammar Accord:
Help Nouns and Pronouns Agree

If you remember early grammar lessons, you might recall
learning that **a *noun* is a person, place or thing**:
man | village | car
The *man* drove to a nearby *village* to test-drive the *car*.

**A *proper noun* takes the place of a noun; it is a
specific person, place or thing:**
John | Mayville | Chevrolet
John drove to *Mayville* to test-drive the *Chevrolet*.

**A *pronoun* takes the place of or refers to a noun; it
generally is less specific than a noun or proper noun:**
he, you, they, it, ours, who, which, anyone, that, this, those.
He drove *there* to test-drive *it*.

Pronouns can get us into grammatical trouble when
they don't "agree" with the noun they represent.

**Here are samples of mismatched nouns
and pronouns, along with potential rewrites:**

mismatch: *Whoever* (singular) breaks the rules is going to find *they* (plural) will be penalized.
better: *Whoever* breaks the rules will find out there are penalties.

mismatch: *A patient* (singular) should feel comfortable with *their* (plural) physician.
better: *Patients* should feel comfortable with *their* physician.

mismatch: Most experts say that as *a baby* (singular) grows and matures, *they* (plural) start sleeping longer at night.
better: Most experts say that as *babies* grow and mature, *they* start sleeping longer at night.

These "one" pronouns often create problems with subject/verb agreement:
everyone | anyone | someone

mismatch: *Everyone* (every single person) may use *their* (multiple persons) computers during class.
better: *All* students may use computers during class.

mismatch: *Anyone* (any one person) who rides a bicycle should wear *their* (multiple persons) helmet.
better: *Anyone* who rides a bicycle should wear a helmet.

mismatch: If you see *someone* (one person) using the back door, please direct *them* (multiple persons) to the front.
better: If you see *people* using the back door, please direct *them* to the front.

✓ **Killer Tip:** The words *everybody, anybody, anyone, each, neither, nobody* and *someone* are considered singular and should be paired with singular pronouns. Some believe *they* is becoming an acceptable pairing. I'm not yet among them.

17

One Word or Two:
Use Care With Your Shortcuts

What's wrong with this headline:

How to Setup a Marketing Campaign
To Capture More Leads

If you recognized ***setup*** as incorrect (it should be ***set up***), good for you! You're a better grammarian than the person who wrote the headline.

When a verb such as *set* is used with a preposition such as *up*, it is called a phrasal verb: *set up*. Combining a verb with an adverb also creates a phrasal verb: *cut back*.

But when the elements of the phrasal verb are combined and expressed as one word, they create a noun: *setup*, *cutback*, *breakdown*

Each of the following examples has two sentences. The first uses a phrasal verb (two words), and the second uses a noun — a single word created by a verb and a preposition. (Exception: *cut* in No. 4 is followed by the adverb *back*.)

► Please arrive early to set *up* the room.
► *Setup* should be done by 3 o'clock.

► Guests must *check out* before 11 a.m.
► *Checkout* is 11 a.m.

► We had to *clean up* the pavilion after the picnic.
► *Cleanup* didn't begin until late afternoon.

► We're going to have to get more exercise and *cut back* on desserts.
► If you want to lose weight, calorie *cutback* should be part of your plan.

► Businesses that *start up* with too little capital often fail.
► The *startup* required SBA financing.

► You can *sign up* for the seminar in room 208.
► Seminar *signup* ended last week.

► I *back up* my computer daily.
► Do you use the cloud for computer *backup*?

► Please *break down* the price by material, labor and profit.
► What kind of price *breakdown* did she provide?

► He's going to *fall out* of favor with his boss if he misses more work.
► He got fired — the *fallout* of missing too much work.

► If you can *stand by* for a later flight, you'll get a free fare.
► If you have a flexible schedule, flying *standby* can save you money.

✓ **Killer Tip:** When you take a *shortcut* and combine words, take care not to *cut short* the accuracy of your message.

18

Take a Peek and Be Piqued: Check Your Word IQ

The English language has words that are pronounced the same — *peek*, *peak* and *pique*, for example — but are spelled differently and have different meanings.

We have words that derive from the same root word and have meanings that differ just slightly: *uninterested* and *disinterested*, for example.

We have words with seemingly common elements — similar spelling and pronunciation such as *elude, allude* and *delude* — but have different meanings.

Here's a sampler of words that are easy to confuse and thus easy to misuse.

Sound the same
- ▶ **peek**: *to peer from a place of concealment.* He peeked through the hole in the fence.
- ▶ **peak**: *highest level or point, or a projecting end.* He reached the peak of the mountain. When he leaned to kiss her, the peak of his cap bumped her forehead.

► **pique**: *to irritate or excite.* Ali was piqued by his refusal of her invitation. The sale piqued his interest in a suit.

Same root word
► **uninterested**: *having no interest or personal concern.* Despite her culinary skills, Beth was uninterested in entering the baking contest.
► **disinterested**: *neutral, impartial.* We sought a disinterested chef from another town to judge our local baking contest.

Seem similar, but different meanings
► **elude**: *to avoid or escape.* He eluded the police.
► **allude**: *to refer to something.* As he questioned the suspect, the officer alluded to a neighborhood bank that had just been robbed.
► **delude**: *to mislead or deceive.* The suspect deluded police by having his sister vouch for his whereabouts at the time of the robbery.

► **assure**: *to give confidence; to remove doubt or anxiety.* Please assure me that you'll deposit the check by noon.
► **ensure**: *to guarantee.* I'll use my iPhone's mobile banking app to ensure that the check is deposited by noon.
► **insure**: *refers to insurance.* I insure my house, car and antiques.

► **detract**: *to reduce or take away the worth or value of.* The poor grammar he used detracted from his credibility.
► **distract**: *to draw away or divert; to disturb concentration.* I was so distracted by the cellphone conversation next to me, I couldn't concentrate on my book.

✓ **Killer Quote:** "If the English language made any sense, *lackadaisical* would have something to do with a shortage of flowers." — Doug Larson

19

Careless Qualifiers Can Diminish Your Credibility

A qualifier is a word or phrase that typically expresses degree or intensity. It can show how certain or absolute a statement is — or isn't.

Two overused qualifiers — *sort of* and *kind of* — pervade today's conversations, but they rarely add meaning or clarification. In fact, they weaken a message.

Consider how qualifiers soften these messages:
▶ I felt *kind of* sad to watch my favorite candidate stumble during the debate.
▶ Williams *sort of* dominated the tennis match.
▶ Ian *kind of* got tangled up in the rope, and then he got *sort of* furious about it.
▶ I was *sort of* devastated when I found out that she had lied to me.
▶ Jason is *kind of* passionate about fly-fishing.

Consider the statements *without* the qualifiers:
▶ I felt sad to watch my favorite candidate stumble during the debate.
▶ Williams dominated the tennis match.

- Ian got tangled up in the rope, and then he got furious about it.
- I was devastated when I found out that she had lied to me.
- Jason is passionate about fly-fishing.

Can you be *slightly* devastated? *Somewhat* passionate? A *little bit* furious?

When referring to strong emotions, there are no degrees; you either are devastated, passionate or furious, or you are not.

When qualifiers can help

If you truly want to dilute or soften a statement, a qualifier can help:

- I was *kind of* disappointed in your work on the annual report.
- Don't you think it's *sort of* late to be calling for a dinner reservation?
- She felt *kind of* hurt that he didn't call, but she realized his predicament.

The next time you see a talk-show guest interviewed or listen to a panel discuss any topic, note the number of times you hear *sort of* and *kind of.* These qualifiers, when used repeatedly, become distracting.

✓ **Killer Tip:** You risk diminishing your authority and credibility by overusing qualifiers. Don't *kind of* or *sort of* anything unless your intention is to soften your message or appear less than certain.

20

Redundancy Rant:
A Dozen Redundancies to Avoid

We are so bombarded by messages — tweets, texts, emails, phone calls, news reports, billboards, neon signs — that every unnecessary word adds to the communication clutter our minds must process.

Most redundancies are the result of careless writing or speaking. If you're uncertain about your redundancy quotient, pick a friend or colleague and listen for a week to each other's extra — and unnecessary — words.

Here are 12 examples of common redundancies from a variety of sources:

1. He made a rapid departure ~~away~~ from his previous statement.
2. Regional water supplies have been dwindling ~~down~~ for years.
3. It's his own fault for allowing the opportunity to be snatched ~~away~~ from him.
4. She was good at masking ~~over~~ her true feelings.
5. Let's separate ~~out~~ the best ideas for conference topics.
6. The event gave staff scattered around the country a chance to meet ~~together~~ face to face.

7. The temperature will drop ~~down~~ 10 degrees tomorrow.
8. The community had been warned ~~in advance~~ to prepare for the storm.
9. How much regulatory power should the new committee strip ~~away~~ from the Federal Reserve?
10. Is your life returning ~~back~~ to normal after your surgery?
11. He has not had any income ~~coming in~~ for over a year.
12. **And the redundancy I hear every day at some point:** He told me the **exact same** story two weeks ago. (Either *exact story* or *same story* would suffice.)

To speak and write like a pro, clean up the clutter by cutting redundancies.

✓ **Killer Quote:** "Clutter is the disease of American writing. We are a society strangling in unnecessary words, circular constructions, pompous frills and meaningless jargon." — William Zinsser

21

What Do Similes Say?
What's a Metaphor For?

Similes and metaphors enrich our writing and speaking by painting word pictures. They add life and color. Here are examples of each.

A *simile* compares two fundamentally unlike things and often is introduced by *like* or *as:*
▶ Her belt was like a snake curling around her waist.
▶ His hair was as dry and brittle as a haystack.
▶ She tried to run, but her legs were like rubber.

A *metaphor* is a word or phrase that names or describes an object by implying a likeness or analogy:
▶ Her belt was a snake curling around her waist.
▶ His dry, brittle hair was a haystack.
▶ She tried to run, but her legs were rubber.

These examples have either a simile or a metaphor. Can you identify which is which?
▶ New York City's population is as diverse as a patchwork quilt.
▶ New York City's population is a patchwork quilt.

▶ Her razor criticism cut his ego to shreds.
▶ Her criticism was as sharp as a razor, cutting his ego to shreds.

▶ He has survived the ups and downs of his roller-coaster life.
▶ His life has been like a roller coaster, but he has managed to survive the ups and downs.

✓ **Killer Tip:** A simile has the letters *l (like)* and *s (as)*. A metaphor has neither.

Answers to last set of examples:
▶ patchwork quilt: simile, then metaphor
▶ razor criticism: metaphor, then simile
▶ roller coaster life: metaphor, then simile

22

That vs. Who:
VIPs Share Grammar Faux Pas

"I'm sorry there's at least one of my colleagues that
can't take a joke."
— Sen. John McCain dissing Sen. Chuck Schumer

"You have a president that's got your back."
— President Barack Obama to Native American
tribal leaders

Generally, *who* is preferred when referring to people.
Sen. McCain and President Obama won't get arrested
by the grammar police, but I'm always disappointed
when a highly visible and well-educated public figure
uses nonstandard grammar.

Who is preferred when referring to human beings.
▶ Sen. Chuck Schumer was the person ~~that~~ *who*
couldn't take a joke.
▶ President Barack Obama assured Native American
leaders, "You have a president ~~that's~~ *who*'s got your
back."

- Anyone ~~that~~ *who* wants to excel at swimming must practice every day.
- The quarterback ~~that~~ *who* threw an interception regrets his actions.

That is preferred for animals without names.

- The dog *that* showed up at our door was mangy and thin.
- The kitten *that* was cold and wet looked pathetic.

Who is preferred for animals with names.

- Rover, the dog *who* showed up at our door, was mangy and thin.
- Boots, the kitten *who* was cold and wet, looked pathetic.

✓ **Killer Tip:** Just because prominent figures such as a senator and a president get a little careless with grammar, it doesn't give the rest of us a pass. I encourage you to mind you grammar p's and q's — and your *thats* and *whos*.

23

There's Something You Should Know About There's

What's wrong with these statements:
▶ There is three things I need to get done this morning.
▶ There is all sorts of circumstances that affect the outcome.
▶ There is times to speak and times to listen.

You don't have to be a grammar scholar to recognize that the verb *is* denotes singular. Each statement refers to multiples, so each should have started *There are*.

So what about these statements:
▶ There's three things I need to get done this morning.
▶ There's all sorts of circumstances that affect the outcome.
▶ There's times to speak and times to listen.

There's is the contraction for *There is*, not *There are*. Each of these sentences refers to multiple things, so each is grammatically incorrect. *There are three things ... There are all sorts ... There are times ...* are correct.

Yet the contraction *there's* often is universally applied to *there is* and *there are* statements. Based on my observations, I suspect we'd more often hear the incorrect *there's* used in each of these examples than the correct *there are*.

Some sources consider *there're* an appropriate contraction for *there are*, but it is difficult to say and looks odd when written. I recommend avoiding it.

✓ **Killer Tip:** I nominate *there's* as the most-misused contraction of our time. Start listening for *there's* when it should be *there are*, and try to avoid being among those who take this incorrect shortcut.

24

Fuzzy Reporting: Is It Titled or Entitled?

A bizarre CNN news report appearing online and on television described 100 malformed or damaged human brains found in a closet at the University of Texas, Austin.

The photographer who made the discovery decided to publish a book about the brains — with photos, of course. According to the CNN online report:

> But even as he was photographing them for a book entitled "malformed", he was hearing that half of the collection was missing and curators were speculating about where they went.

Overlooking that the title *Malformed* should be capitalized and the comma should go inside the closing quotation mark, *entitled* is used incorrectly: "a book entitled ..." It should be "a book titled ..."

Entitled means a right to do or to have something:
▶ After spending the morning cleaning the garage, Ethan was entitled to a nap.
▶ Susan has worked hard and is entitled to a promotion.

Titled **has to do with the name of something — a book, poem, movie or work of art, for example:**

▶ John Steinbeck won a Pulitzer Prize for fiction with his novel titled *Grapes of Wrath*.

▶ A television program titled *Game of Thrones* continues to gain in popularity.

Former *Late Night* host David Letterman consistently announced his show's musical entertainment by citing the individual's or group's CD as being "entitled," followed by its name.

I wish highly paid entertainers, who because of their success and visibility are role models, would pay more attention to grammar.

I wish the same for reporters, whose reputations and whose news outlets' reputations are on the line.

✓ **Killer Tip:** Whether you're writing or speaking about a book, a television program or a CD, not one is *entitled;* all are *titled.* Let's use our brains to get it right.

25

To *s* or Not To *s:* That Is the Question

Do you say or write:
- ▶ He walked *toward* (or *towards?*) the lake.
- ▶ She stepped backward (or backwards?) and stumbled off the porch.
- ▶ Let's move forward (or forwards?) with our plan.

Many sources say either works, but most suggest no *s* with *toward, backward* or *forward* in American English.

Reminder: Don't confuse *forward*, a direction of movement, with *foreword*, a short introductory statement for a book or other published work.

The Queen's English
If you are from Great Britain or have clients in the U.K., you likely know that *towards* is the preferred usage there:

- ▶ The Queen's limousine is heading *towards* Buckingham Palace.
- ▶ The Scotland Yard investigator said the case was moving *towards* a conclusion.

What about anyway or anyways?

Again, common usage in the United States does not include the *s:*

▶ If it rains, we'll take a walk *anyway*.
▶ She wasn't home, but we left the package *anyway*.

And how about outdoor or outdoors?

In this case, there is a difference. *Outdoor* is an adjective, and *outdoors* is a noun:

Adjective

▶ She enjoyed *outdoor* activities such as fishing and hunting.
▶ Let's look for a restaurant that offers *outdoor* dining.

Noun

▶ He prefers a job that allows him to work *outdoors*.
▶ It should be warm enough *outdoors* this evening for patio dining.

✓ **Killer Tip:** Adding an *s* will not impair understanding of toward, backward, forward or anyway, but eliminating it in these cases reflects the standard U.S. English no-*s* convention.

26

Were vs. Was in *Fiddler on the Roof*

If you've seen *Fiddler on the Roof* — or even if you haven't — you might be familiar with the famous musical's popular song "If I Were a Rich Man."

Tevye, the leading character in the musical, laments his lowly position as a milkman, but he considers what becoming wealthy could bring: a fine house, esteem and respect in his community, and a better life for his wife and five daughters.

were vs. was
Notice that the lyrics are not "If I **was** a rich man," a word choice that unfortunately seems to be on the rise.

▶ If Tevye *used to be rich*, he would sing:
   When I *was* a rich man …
▶ If he is counting on *becoming rich*, he would sing:
   When I *am* a rich man …

Using *If* expresses a condition he wishes for but is contrary to fact at present; he's envisioning what life *would* be like *if he were rich*.

Present, past, future vs. subjective / hypothetical

Were conveys what is known as the *subjunctive* mood; *were* is conditional, hypothetical, a wished-for state, something contrary to fact.

Revisiting the *rich* example:

I am rich now. I was rich yesterday. I have been rich for years, and I will be rich tomorrow. But if I am *not* rich, I can speak only in terms of wishing I *were* rich.

Here are examples of how *if* implies the hypothetical:

► If I were you, I'd buy a new car rather than repair the old one.

► If he were smart, he'd call his brother and apologize.

► If the knife were sharper, it would be easier to dice onions.

Here are other examples of the hypothetical:

► Her acting is so convincing, you'd think she were living her life onstage.

► The dog gulped the food as if it were his first meal in weeks.

► The principal wishes he were retiring in the spring.

✓ **Killer Tip:** It might be conversational to say, "If I *was* polite, I wouldn't correct your grammar." But conversational doesn't have to mean ungrammatical.

✓ **Bonus Killer Tip:** A teacher friend always used this memorable advertising jingle as an example for her students: "If I *were* an Oscar Mayer wiener, everyone would be in love with me."

ABBREVIATIONS

and

CAPITALIZATIONS

Why is "abbreviation" such a long word?

— Unknown

27

Abbreviations vs. Acronyms: What's the Difference?

Abbreviations (also called initialisms) that substitute for multiple words are shortcuts to express long, sometimes complicated or hard-to-remember terms. They take less space as well as less time to write and to say. In speaking, we pronounce each individual letter of an abbreviation:

ATM: Automated Teller Machine
CDC: Centers for Disease Control and Prevention
CIA: Central Intelligence Agency
EPA: Environmental Protection Agency
FBI: Federal Bureau of Investigation
GMO: genetically modified organism
HMO: Health Maintenance Organization
LED: light-emitting diode

Acronyms also are created from first letters of words, but they are pronounced as a single word:

ANSI: American National Standards Institute
laser: light amplification by stimulated emission of radiation
LEED: Leadership in Energy and Environmental Design

NASA: National Aeronautics and Space Administration
NATO: North Atlantic Treaty Organization
OPEC: Organization of Petroleum Producing Countries
OSHA: Occupational Safety and Health Administration
STEM: Science, Technology, Engineering, Math
scuba: self-contained underwater breathing apparatus

Although many abbreviations and acronyms are universally recognized, it's always considerate to write out anything that might not be familiar to readers. In a second reference and beyond, using just the abbreviation is appropriate.

> The Centers for Disease Control and Prevention has issued warnings about the coming season's flu epidemic. This is the second consecutive year the CDC has warned residents.

The AP Stylebook suggests avoiding the practice of putting abbreviations in parentheses:

> The Centers for Disease Control and Prevention (CDC) has issued warnings about this season's flu epidemic. This is the second consecutive year the CDC has warned residents.

The style guide explains:
Do not follow an organization's full name with an abbreviation or acronym in parentheses or set off by dashes. If an abbreviation or acronym would not be clear on second reference without this arrangement, do not use it.

✓ **Killer Tip:** If an abbreviation starts with a letter pronounced as a vowel sound, it requires the article *an* rather than *a:* an FBI staff member, an LED product, an HMO requirement.

28

True or False:
Always Capitalize Bible and God

When I wrote in a post on my blog that The Associated Press Stylebook was my primary resource for word and punctuation use — in other words, my bible — a reader suggested that I should have capitalized bible.

Had I been referring to the Bible that contains what we commonly call the Scriptures — Christian writings that include the Old and New Testaments — I would have capitalized it.

But I was not referring to *that* Bible.

Neither Bible nor God has to — nor should — be capitalized in every use. Not capitalizing them doesn't mean that you're irreverent or breaking a written-in-stone grammatical or religious rule.

▶ The Associated Press Stylebook is my grammar bible.
▶ Some say that *Business Adventures* by John Brookes is a bible for billionaires.
▶ Is there a bible for sales reps?

When you refer to a figure that is the God of any monotheistic religion — a religion that recognizes only one God — you capitalize it.

Christianity, Judaism and Islam all are considered religions with one God.

There are many polytheistic religions in the world, faiths that have multiple gods that represent different beliefs, values, myths and legends. The Asatru religion, for example, has many Norse gods and goddesses.

Not all god references have a religious component:
▶ It was sad to see him worship money as his god.
▶ We are godparents for our best friends' daughter.
▶ Ye gods! (an exclamation of astonishment)

✓ **Killer Tip:** As The Ruthless Editor, I never mind being challenged or questioned; I learn with each query that comes my way. If you answered True to this chapter heading's True/False question, I hope you've learned and welcomed the lesson as well.

29

Four Common Latin Abbreviations Clarified

We call Italian, French, Spanish and Portuguese the Romance languages, not because these populations are known for love and courting, but because as the Roman Empire expanded, its culture and language — Latin — influenced them.

Romanice, an adjective that suggested "in the Roman Manner," over time was shortened to *Romance*. Capitalizing it as *Romance language* clarifies its connotation of Roman influence.

Here are four common abbreviations with Latin roots.

1. i.e. The Latin *id est* means *that is* or *in other words*. Use *i.e.* either to explain or to clarify by listing options or rephrasing a previous statement. It fits with many forms of punctuation — parentheses, a semicolon or dashes — and generally is followed by a comma.

▶ Our country's three West Coast states (i.e., California, Oregon and Washington) have ocean views that draw visitors from around the world.

- I told Ella to stop by close to noon to meet our new client; i.e., she doesn't need an appointment.
- I'm taking Ryan's dinner to him — i.e., I'll be driving across town this evening — so let me know if you need anything from the market.

2. e.g. From the Latin expression *exempli gratia*, e.g. means *for example*. It, too, should be followed by a comma.

- On the East Coast, cherry trees reach full bloom in late March; e.g., March 25 marked this season's peak.
- The magazine will print articles that support its mission: e.g., stories about career change or major life transitions.
- I sometimes hesitate to make editorial corrections (e.g., making a singular noun and pronoun agree) where ungrammatical use has become the norm. Here's a common error: "*Sears* has said *they*'ll refund the purchase" should read "*Sears* has said *it* will refund the purchase."

3. et al. This abbreviation derives from the Latin *et alii*, meaning *and others*. It does not require a comma. And for the record, there is a feminine and a gender-neutral form (*et alii* is considered masculine), but I try to keep things simple. We often see *et al.* used in bibliographies when referring to multiple authors.

- Watson, Kathleen et al. *Killer Tips from The Ruthless Editor and Her Band of Grumpy Grammarians*. New York: McGraw Hill, 2016.
- Technology companies Apple, Microsoft, Google et al. have a relaxed dress code that appeals to young workers.
- The mayor, his staff, city council members et al. will be in transition for several weeks following the election.

Et al. also stands for *et alibi*, a less common usage meaning *elsewhere*.

4. etc. Probably the most common of the Latin abbreviations, *etc.* stands for *et cetera* and means *and the rest* or *and so forth*. It should be preceded by a comma.

Good writing should not leave the reader with unanswered questions, so *etc.* should be used sparingly. However, it works here:

> We will serve a variety of cold beverages at the picnic: soda, lemonade, iced tea, etc.

✓ **Killer Tip: Here's how I remember what each abbreviation stands for:**
i.e. — means *in other words* (both *i.e.* and *in* start with *i*).
e.g. — means *for eggs-ample* (OK, it's hokey, but it works for me.)
et al. — is close to *and all;* the period signifies that *all* have been included. Period. The end.
etc. — is so common that no memory aid is needed.

30

Academic Degrees: Words or Letters?

Using periods with academic degrees is changing. For now, Associated Press style still includes them in most cases.

- ▶ Bachelor of Arts/Science (B.A./B.S.)
- ▶ bachelor's degree (but associate degree: no 's)

- ▶ Master of Arts/Science (M.A./M.S.)
- ▶ Master of Fine Arts (MFA)
- ▶ Master of Science in Social Work (MSW)
- ▶ Master of Business Administration (MBA)
- ▶ master's degree

- ▶ Doctor of Philosophy (Ph.D.)
- ▶ Doctor of Medicine (M.D.)
- ▶ Doctor of Dental Surgery (DDS)

If you add *degree* to any of the above, use lowercase: He earned his M.S. degree in May. Use lowercase when the degree field is generic: She earned her master's last year.

✓ **Killer Tip:** When an academic abbreviation is used after a name, set it off by commas: "Speaker Jay Brown, Ph.D., opened the meeting. Sue White, M.S., followed."

31

Honor Parents, But Do It Right

Every spring, we're bookended by holidays that honor parenthood: Mother's Day, which is the second Sunday in May, and Father's Day, which is the third Sunday in June.

Some people, wanting to show respect for parents, always capitalize any form of mom or dad.

Regardless of our desire to demonstrate that we respect and cherish our parents, there are times to capitalize and times to use lowercase. Here is a simple guideline to help you choose:

If a parent's name could replace your mom or dad in your phrasing, use capitals. If not, use lowercase:

▶ I told Mom (Jean) I'd be home by midnight.
▶ I told my mom (~~my Jean~~) I'd be home by midnight.

In the second example, you of course would not say, "I told my Jean I'd be home by midnight."

Here are two more examples:

▶ Dad (Frank) is going to coach the soccer team.
▶ My dad (~~My Frank~~) is going to coach the soccer team.

Again, you wouldn't say, "My Frank is going to coach the soccer team."

Expressing gratitude and honoring your mom and dad is always appropriate and appreciated, regardless of the time of year.

✓ **Killer Tip:** For grandparents, aunts and uncles, follow these examples:
  ▶ My grandma and grandpa just arrived.
  ▶ Grandma and Grandpa just arrived. (You could substitute their names.)
  ▶ Grandma Joyce and Grandpa Jim just arrived. (Capitalize these terms when they are used as a title before a name.)
  ▶ His aunt and uncle live nearby.
  ▶ Aunt Becky and Uncle Josh live nearby. (Aunt and Uncle here are titles.)

32

Leave Postal Abbreviations Out of Your Prose

In October 1963, the United States Postal Service introduced five-digit ZIP codes to follow the state name in the last line of a mailing address. To make room for the ZIP Code, it also issued two-letter abbreviations for all U.S. states and territories.

As digital communication and social media opened the door to the need for condensed messages, the two-letter representations began making their way into all kinds of writing.

Is that a problem? Take this quick quiz:
▶ Does AL mean Alabama or Alaska?
▶ Does AR mean Arizona or Arkansas?
▶ Does CO mean Connecticut or Colorado?
▶ Does ID mean Idaho or Indiana?
▶ Does MA mean Massachusetts, Maine or Maryland?
▶ Does MI mean Missouri, Mississippi, Michigan or Minnesota?
▶ Does MO mean Montana, Minnesota or Missouri?
▶ Does NE mean Nebraska or Nevada?

If you hail from one of these states or send mail to one of them frequently, you quickly picked out the correct match.

But if you had to pause to figure out if MI is Michigan, Minnesota, Missouri or Mississippi — or if you are from a country other than the Unites States — you probably had to look it up.

The growth of global communication and international business has rendered two-letter abbreviations outdated in prose. The AP Stylebook now recommends full state names in the body of a story or document. Two-letter postal code representations belong *only* in mailing addresses.

There are some exceptions:
In lists, tables, charts or tabular material, you might consider still using abbreviations. If so, stick to the pre-postal code system. For example:

▶ Ala. for Alabama
▶ Minn. for Minnesota
▶ Nev. for Nevada

Political affiliations also can be abbreviated:
▶ Sen. John McCain, R-Ariz.
▶ Gov. Jerry Brown, D-Calif.
▶ Rep. Barbara Comstock, R-Va.

✓ **Killer Tip:** Making clear to your international business associates or customers that you don't expect them to memorize all 50 two-letter state abbreviations is more about courtesy than shortcuts.

33

Seasons, Regions, Directions: Which Do You Capitalize?

Almost everyone pays attention to the weather. We know that storms generally travel west to east, and we know that weather changes by the season. So when it comes to seasons, regions and directions, what needs to be capitalized?

Seasons generally are not capitalized:
▶ After a punishing winter, everyone hopes for an early spring.
▶ As youngsters, we spent lazy summers at the lake.

But capitalize a season when it's part of the name of an event:
▶ We're looking forward to attending Winter Wonderfest at Navy Pier in Chicago.
▶ Purdue holds a fitness walk during its Spring Fling weekend.

Directions and parts of the country aren't quite as clear-cut.

Don't capitalize north, south, east or west when describing a compass direction:

▶ Sam is heading east as soon as he finishes his final exams.

▶ Tiffany found her phone at the north entrance of the building.

Don't capitalize a general area of a state or city:

▶ Danielle hopes to buy a ranch somewhere in western Montana.

▶ They operate an Airbnb on the eastern edge of Portland.

Do capitalize specific regions of a country or of the world:

▶ Amy works in the Pacific Northwest, but her new job will take her to the Far East.

▶ Josh expanded his Midwest company's reach to East Coast and Pacific Rim countries.

Do capitalize a region or location when it is part of a proper noun:

▶ Will Santa fly over the South Pole on his way to Wisconsin's North Woods?

▶ The entire Western Hemisphere is in the middle of an unprecedented deep freeze.

✓ **Killer Tip:** In general, don't capitalize seasons or compass directions. Do capitalize specific regions as well as a region or location that is part of a proper noun.

PUNCTUATION

Let eat Grandma!
Let's eat, Grandma!

Punctuation saves lives!

34

Accent Marks and Other Symbols

If you conduct business internationally, your customers will be impressed and find it helpful if you know how to use certain standard accent marks.

Even if you don't have international clients, you likely have multicultural friends or colleagues for whom these marks have meaning.

Here are five fairly common marks that, for our purposes, I'm going to consider punctuation. Some have implications in physics and math as well, but we'll consider their use only with words or letters. They determine how something is pronounced.

1. Tilde
The tilde is the wavy line that goes above the *n* in some words, often those of Spanish or Portuguese origin.
You likely know the pronunciation implication: the tilde introduces a nyah sound:
mun-YA-nuh, pin-YA-tuh, sen-YOR
mañana | piñata | señor

Acute and Grave Accents

Two marks — acute and grave — most often are used with words of French derivation. Here's the first:

2. Acute accent: same angle as backslash / makes *ay* sound

résumé | cliché | fiancé (male) or fiancée (female)

3. Grave accent: same angle as forward slash \ makes *eh* sound

après (after) ski | très (very) fatigued | frère (brother)

When used with letters other than e, the grave accent does not indicate a sound difference but rather distinguishes a different meaning for a word. For example, the menu phrase *à la carte* translates to "from the menu." Items under this heading can be ordered individually.

4. Cedilla

A symbol that resembles a small comma attached to the bottom curve of a *c*, the cedilla gives the *c* a "soft" or *s* sound rather than a hard *k* sound:

façade (front or face of building) | garçon (boy) | français (French)

5. Umlaut

The two dots above an *a*, *o* or *u* in German words create different sounds when pronounced and thus different meanings among words spelled the same or nearly the same.

A common use of the umlaut in English is *über*, which means highest, greatest, most extreme example of. Pronounce über not like the oo in who, but as though it is spelled eu-ber; include a hint of e — eeeuuwww, as though you've just caught a whiff of something stinky.

Using über in English:
über-comfortable | über-nerd Bill Gates | über-hip new restaurant

This is by no means an exhaustive list of accent marks or their use, nor does it show every use of every mark mentioned.

It does, however, cover some fairly common non-English-derived words that we have adopted and hear often among English-speaking people.

Miscellaneous Marks
These marks considered punctuation are not covered elsewhere in this book:

Ampersand: &
The ampersand is acceptable when it's part of a company's name (Procter & Gamble), but generally avoid it as a substitute for *and* except in common abbreviations such as B&B (Bed and Breakfast) or R&B (Rhythm and Blues).

Asterisk: * (pronounced AS ter isk)
An asterisk placed at the end a word or phrase* in content indicates that the reader should check the bottom of that page for additional information.

When an asterisk comes at the end of sentence, place it outside of the punctuation marks.*

Percent Sign: %
Write out *percent* in most cases, but use numbers for the quantity:
► The committee agreed to spend 30 percent of the landscape budget on new trees.
► Barely a majority of students — just 52 percent — passed the final exam.

The symbol might be more appropriate in tabular material or where space is limited. Technical publication style guides might prefer the symbol %:

▶ Over 90% of the loans were repaid in full.

▶ The cost breakdown was 55% raw material, 12% labor, 6% shipping, and the balance general overhead.

When the percentage is considered singular, it takes a singular verb. When the percentage is considered plural, it takes a plural verb:

▶ Only 40 percent of the committee plans to attend the meeting.

▶ Only 40 percent of committee members plan to attend the meeting.

✓ **Killer Tip**: See *The Mac is Not a typewriter* and *The PC is Not a typewriter* by Robin Williams for shortcuts in creating these and other marks. Or check this link that shows how to insert special characters when using Microsoft Word: http://bit.ly/1neKOhL

35

Avoid Apostrophe When Noun Is Descriptive, Not Possessive

Inserting an apostrophe can indicate there is possession involved. These examples show that what might appear to be possessive simply is descriptive. Which are correct?

Which of these is correct?
▶ United Mine Workers Health & Pension Plan
▶ United Mine Worker's Health & Pension Plan
▶ United Mine Workers' Health & Pension Plan

▶ a teachers college
▶ a teacher's college
▶ a teachers' college

▶ a Mac users help group
▶ a Mac user's help group
▶ a Mac users' help group

In each case, the first example is correct. *United Mine Workers* and *teachers* and *Mac users* all describe rather than show possession:

► The mine workers don't own the plan; they subscribe to it.
► The teachers don't own the college; they attend it.
► The Mac users don't own the group; they participate in it.

In general, apply this guideline:
An apostrophe usually is not added if *for* or *by* rather than *of* would be appropriate in the longer form:
► the Health & Pension Plan *for* members of the United Mine Workers
► a college *for* teachers
► a help group *for* Mac users

Here are other examples where someone might be tempted to make the noun a plural possessive when it is simply descriptive:
► the nurses station (a station *for* nurses)
► a Chicago Bears lineman (a lineman *for* the Bears)
► a writers guide (a guide *for* writers)

✓ **Killer Tip:** Spellcheck does not accurately discern every potential use of the apostrophe. Use care with these and similar descriptive terms.

36

Yours, Mine and Ours: Individual vs. Joint Possession

When two people jointly own something, placing the apostrophe can be tricky.

The dilemma: one apostrophe or two?
► I stopped by Brad and Kim's house.
► I stopped by Brad's and Kim's house.

What about this construction?
► The shelves held Eric and Laura's books.
► The shelves held Eric's and Laura's books.

In the first example, Brad and Kim share ownership of the same house, so the first sentence using just one apostrophe is correct: Brad and Kim's house.

In the second example, Eric's collection of books is different from Laura's collection, so the second sentence using two apostrophes is correct: Eric's and Laura's books.

Here are other correct examples:
► Adam and Kari's Irish Setters
   (two dogs, shared ownership)

► Adam's and Kari's golf clubs
  (two sets of clubs, individual ownership)
► Craig's and Brooke's motorcycles
  (two motorcycles, individual ownership)
► Craig and Brooke's yard
  (one yard, shared ownership)

Ownership with pronouns

When you are using *my*, *his* or *hers*, follow these examples:
► The Realtor wanted to tour *my* and Brad's house.
  (not *me* and Brad's house)
► She also wanted to tour *his* and Kim's house.
  (not *he* and Kim's house)
► We decided to tour *her* and Brad's house.
  (not *she* and Brad's house)

Test the *me/my, he/his, she/her* dilemma by simply eliminating the second person.

► They wanted to tour me ~~and Brad's~~ house.
  They wanted to tour *my* house.
► They wanted to tour his ~~and Kim's~~ house.
  They wanted to tour *his* house.
► They wanted to tour she ~~and Brad's~~ house.
  They wanted to tour *her* house.

Other common errors to avoid:

► Let's stop by ~~him~~ *his* and *Kim's* house this afternoon.
► Please drop by ~~mine~~ *my* and Brad's house this evening.

✓ **Killer Tip:** We're often more relaxed when speaking than when writing, because we can read body language to be sure we're being understood. Yet it's always helpful to know what's correct so we can decide how informal we want to be or what kind of an impression we want to make.

37

Using Apostrophes
With Letters and Words

The apostrophe helps us form contractions (what's new),
shows us that something is missing (rock 'n' roll), and
helps us create possessives and plurals.

Here's how to correctly use apostrophes with plurals of
letters and words.

**When you have a single letter (lowercase or capital)
that you want to make plural, add an apostrophe:**
- ▶ Mind your p's and q's.
- ▶ He reviewed the contract to be sure he had
  dotted all the i's and crossed all the t's.
- ▶ The Oakland A's play the Minnesota Twins
  on Saturday.

**When you have multiple capital letters, do not add
an apostrophe:**
- ▶ She knew her ABCs by the time she started
  nursery school.
- ▶ Four VIPs joined Prince Charles in his box
  seat at the opera.
- ▶ Someone vandalized all of the bank's ATMs.

Exception: If the capital letters are intended to show possession, add an apostrophe:

▶ The VIP's wallet disappeared from her desk drawer.

▶ The ATM's keypad wouldn't work.

▶ NASA's budget will be cut again next year.

When you have a word you want to make plural, generally do not add an apostrophe:

▶ He cluttered his presentation with too many *ands*.

▶ His life is full of regrets about *should-haves*.

▶ How many *pleases* does your child say in a day?

Exceptions:

If making a word plural without an apostrophe might cause confusion for readers, add one. For example, *Thank you's* and *do's and don'ts* need apostrophes. *Yous* could be slang — think of Sylvester Stallone's character Rocky and *yous guys* — and *dos* could be confused with the Spanish word for *two* or for the ancient DOS computer operating system.

✓ **Killer Tip:** What's the origin of p's and q's? One source claims the expression originated in British pubs as an abbreviation for mind your pints and quarts. Another source claims that it originated with printers who set headlines in movable type. Because the lower-case p and q are a mirror image of each other, a reminder to watch your p's and q's meant using care to return them to their correct place after use.

38

Using Apostrophes With Numbers

Now that we know how to use apostrophes with letters and words, let's look at how to use them with numbers.

When you add an *s* to numbers to make them plural, do not add an apostrophe:

► Temperatures dropped into the low 20s last night.
► There were four 727s waiting on the tarmac.
► She said both size 9s were too loose.

When writing about years as decades, do not add an apostrophe:

► She writes regularly about music of the 1960s.
► He spent three years refurbishing a car from the 1940s.
► She found her 1980s cheerleading sweater in the attic.

However, when the year is specific and designates possession, add an apostrophe:

► During 1936's Olympic Games in Berlin, Jesse Owens won four gold medals in track and field events.
► Funds raised this year surpassed 2014's efforts.
► 1929's stock market crash marked the beginning of the Great Depression.

Avoid using numbers to begin a sentence except when the numbers express a year:

2015 was the best year we've had in a decade.

Either write out the number or rewrite the sentence:
wrong: 95 percent of my day is spent responding to emails.
right: Ninety-five percent of my day is spent responding to emails.
right: I spend 95 percent of my day responding to emails.

To summarize, do not use an apostrophe when you are making numbers plural (727s) or when referring to a decade (the 1970s). When you get specific about a particular year with a possessive construction, an apostrophe is appropriate (The Chicago White Sox were 2005's world series champions.)

✓ **Killer Quote**: "I'm writing a book. I've got the page numbers done." — Steven Wright

39

Brackets Add Clarity, Show Errors

Brackets probably are one of the least-used forms of punctuation, but they have their role.

When you put something in parentheses that calls for a second set of parentheses, use brackets instead:

> We have worked with Mercy Hospital since 1995 to provide a number of health benefits to employees. (Our EAP [Employee Assistance Program launched in 2001] is one example.)

Use brackets when you are quoting someone, but it needs clarification. Here, [writing] was added to clarify which campus center stays open:

> "The [writing] center stays open until 10 in the evening for students who need help," she explained.

If original material contains an error — a misspelled word would be an example — use brackets around the Latin term *sic* to indicate that's how it was originally expressed. Translated literally, *sic* means "so, thus, in this manner."

He wrote, "If you think the dog looks funny chasing it's [sic] tail, you should see the cat trying to jump into a paper bag." (*it's* should be *its*)

Here's a quote from a former president known for gaffes. Africa is, of course, a continent, not a nation.

"Africa is a nation [sic] that suffers from incredible disease."

You likely don't need them often, but when something calls for brackets, there is no good substitute.

✓ **Killer Quote:** "Bad grammar makes me [sic]."

— Unknown

40

Should You Capitalize the First Word After a Colon?

The colon comes in handy when you want to provide an example or explanation, to cite a quotation, or to introduce a list. A colon implies that whatever follows it is related to whatever precedes it.

One of the most-asked questions I hear about the colon is whether to capitalize the first word that follows it. Style guides differ, but AP, my preferred source, suggests:

Capitalize the first word after the colon if what follows it constitutes a complete sentence (has a subject and verb):
- ▶ If you want to grow roses, remember this: The soil you plant them in should have a near-neutral pH range.
- ▶ Council members agreed on one point: There will not be a crosswalk at that intersection.
- ▶ He told me the same thing: The class will be offered at the start of the fall semester.

Do not capitalize the first word if the colon is followed by a list or by phrasing that does not form a complete sentence:

► My parents had a hard-and-fast rule: no television until homework was done.
► I need these ingredients for spinach salad: fresh spinach, balsamic vinegar, olive oil, honey, strawberries.
► There are many reasons college freshmen gain weight their first year away from home: stress, dorm food, late-night study snacks, and of course beer.

If you introduce a list with *including*, *namely* or *for instance*, do not use a colon:

► I made a trip to the store to pick up the ingredients I need for spinach salad, including fresh spinach, balsamic vinegar, olive oil, honey and strawberries.
► There are many reasons college freshmen gain weight their first year away from home — namely stress, dorm food, late-night study snacks, and of course beer.

A colon goes outside of quotation marks when it is not part of the quoted element:

► The trainer emphasized three elements of what she called "high-touch service": listening, eye contact and a firm handshake.
► The following musicians may enter the door marked "Backstage": vocalists, keyboardists, percussionists, and guitar and bass players.

✓ **Killer Tip:** Not every source suggests capitalizing the first word of a complete sentence that follows a colon. Choose your preference and be consistent.

41

When Does a Sentence Need a Comma?

The comma is one of the most confusing — and most misused — punctuation marks. Many writers insert a comma where none is needed.

Use a comma to separate two thoughts that could stand alone as sentences.

To create a *complete sentence*, all you need is a subject and a verb:
- ▶ I see.
- ▶ Tad writes.
- ▶ Toby teaches.

A complete sentence can have more than simply a subject and a verb:
- ▶ I see Tad writing on the whiteboard.
- ▶ I see Tad writing on the whiteboard in front of Toby's class.

When you have two complete sentences — two complete thoughts that you want to link using a conjunction (*and, yet, so,* to name a few) — insert a comma between the two sentences:

- ▶ Tad writes poetry. He posts his work online.
- ▶ Tad writes poetry, and he posts his work online.

If you drop the subject *he* that follows *and*, you no longer need the comma, because it no longer can stand alone:

Tad writes poetry and posts his work online.

Here are more examples that show when to include a comma and when to delete it. Note that the first example in each set could be two complete sentences.

- ▶ We appreciate your support, and we hope you'll help again next year.
- ▶ We appreciate your support and hope you'll help again next year.

- ▶ The document describes the rules, yet it still is hard to understand.
- ▶ The document describes the rules yet still is hard to understand.

- ▶ Our corporate team members leave late Sunday, so they will travel all night.
- ▶ Our corporate team members leave late Sunday so will travel all night.

- ✓ **Killer Quote:** "I have been correcting the proofs of my poems. In the morning, after hard work, I took a comma out of one sentence ... in the afternoon, I put it back again." — Oscar Wilde

42

When Does *But* Need a Comma?

But is what we call a *coordinating conjunction*; it connects groups of words that, if they were not connected, could stand alone as complete sentences. The word groups generally are considered equal in importance.

Other common coordinating conjunctions are *and*, *for*, *or*, *nor*, *so* and *yet*.

Some writers wonder whether to *always* use a comma before *but*. The answer: no, not always.

Can you spot what's lacking in the second of each of these examples?

▶ My report was late, but my boss accepted it anyway.
▶ My report was late but was accepted anyway.

▶ I'd like to go to the art fair, but I don't have extra money to spend.
▶ I'd like to go to the art fair but don't have extra money to spend.

▶ Ty was supposed to come to work early, but he forgot.
▶ Ty was supposed to come to work early but forgot.

**The first sentence of each set consists of two complete thoughts that are separated by a comma and *but;* each could be a complete sentence because each has a *subject* and a *verb:*

▶ My report was late. My boss accepted it anyway.
▶ I'd like to go to the art fair. I don't have extra money.
▶ Ty was supposed to come to work early. He forgot.

In the second sentence of each set, what follows has no subject:

... but accepted it anyway.
... but don't have extra money to spend.
... but forgot.

✓ **Killer Tip:** Although the general guideline is to insert a comma before the joiner *but* if the phrase that follows has a *subject* and a *verb*, there can be an exception. If the phrase that follows is an extremely short complete sentence, you might choose to eliminate the comma: Ty was supposed to come to work early but he forgot.

43

Multiple Adjectives Don't Always Need Multiple Commas

When you include multiple adjectives in a sentence, do all of the describing words have to be separated by commas?

The AP Stylebook explains it this way:

Use commas to separate adjectives equal in rank. If the comma could be replaced by the word *and*, the adjectives likely are equal:

▶ She was an *attractive, articulate* spokesperson.

▶ Green bananas have an *unpleasant, bitter* taste.

▶ He drove down a *dark, dangerous* street.

Use no comma when the last adjective before a noun is an integral element of a NOUN PHRASE (multiple words that play the role of a noun):

▶ The spring storm dropped a layer of *fluffy* WHITE SNOW.

▶ He wore a *cheap* COTTON BLAZER.

▶ They honored the *famous* FRENCH WRITER.

A University of Houston-Victoria's "Grammatically Correct" weekly tip explains comma use with adjectives this way:

Overall, there are five classes of descriptive adjectives:
general | age | color | material | origin

When multiple adjectives are from the *same class*, they should be separated by commas:

▶ She was an *attractive, articulate* spokesperson.
attractive, articulate (general)

▶ Their ageless, everlasting love has been an inspiration.
ageless, everlasting (age)

▶ The jutting, razor-edged rocks ended my climb.
jutting, razor-edged (material)

When multiple adjectives are from *different classes*, a comma is not needed.

▶ She was an *articulate elderly British* spokesperson.
articulate (general), *elderly* (age), *British* (origin)

▶ Their *unwavering everlasting* love has been an inspiration.
unwavering (general), *everlasting* (age)

▶ The *insurmountable razor-edged* rocks ended my climb.
insurmountable (general), *razor-edged* (material)

Note that the use of NOUN PHRASE by The AP Stylebook correlates to the University of Houston-Victoria *different class* description; neither requires a comma:

▶ *fluffy* WHITE SNOW — different class adjectives:
fluffy (general), *white* (color), *snow* (noun)

▶ *cheap* COTTON BLAZER — different class adjectives:
cheap (general), *cotton* (material), *blazer* (noun)

▶ *famous* FRENCH WRITER — different class adjectives:
famous (general), *French* (origin), *writer* (noun)

✓ **Killer Tip:** Multiple adjectives are tricky when it comes to commas. Pick which formula is easiest for you to remember and to apply.

44

Should You Make a Dash For It?

Computers give us myriad ways to make our documents attractive, accurate and highly readable.

We all know what a hyphen is: that tiny horizontal line that shows a break in a word that starts on one line and jumps to the next.

> She phoned me during my after-
> noon break, so I missed her call.

Hyphens also join words to clarify meaning or to form a single idea from two or more words: small-business owner, son-in-law, fifty-five.

The hyphen, however, is just one of three horizontal lines that help us communicate clearly. There are two more: the en dash and the em dash.

En Dash
The en dash, so named because it is about as wide as a capital letter N in your chosen font, is used to show duration or span. Use it where you might otherwise use *to:*

- ► Children ages 3 – 5 get in free.
- ► Please bring 2 – 4 dozen cookies to the party.
- ► You'll find the passage on pages 17 – 19.

But avoid using the en dash to show duration when you include word sets *from … to* or *between … and:*
- ► The Korean War lasted from 1950 to 1953
- ► The theater will be open between 10 a.m. and 4 p.m. for a special event.

Em Dash

The em dash, so named because it is about as wide as a capital letter M in your chosen font, is used to show an abrupt change in thought within a sentence or to show an emphatic pause:
- ► I am tired of — or should I say completely disgusted with — the partisanship in Congress.
- ► We will go to New York to see *Hamilton* in May — if my tax refund arrives by then.

An em dash also sets off an author's or composer's name at the end of a quotation:

"Anger is an acid that can do more harm to the vessel in which it is stored than to anything on which it is poured."
— Mark Twain

Don't use a hyphen or an old-fashioned double hyphen to express what really should be a dash.

- ✓ **Killer Quote:** "A dash indeed is quite abrupt. 'Tis put almost to interrupt." — a Lady Teacher in 1854

45

Ellipsis Shows Omission or Thought Trailing Off

There are times in writing or editing when you want to show that something has been omitted from the original version. There also are times when you want to express pauses in a speaker's statement or to indicate that a thought hasn't been completed.

Use the ellipsis — a series of three periods with a space before and after, but no space between each (...) — for such purposes.

Omission

These two examples of online news reports use an ellipsis to show that the second version has been altered:

Original

"Mr. Hayward, whose position is thought to be under threat, risked further fury by continuing plans to pay out a dividend to investors next month."

Edited

"Mr. Hayward ... risked further fury by continuing plans to pay out a dividend to investors next month."

Original

"In the short term, we want these claims to be responded to more quickly," the governor said. "These people need help, and we need to be there to try to make them as whole as we can during this very difficult process."

Edited

"In the short term, we want these claims to be responded to more quickly," the governor said. "These people need help. ... " (The ellipsis following the period indicates the omission.)

Pause or trailing off of thought

In this example, the ellipses indicate pauses in a speaker's statement. An ellipsis implies a pause greater than what would be expressed by a comma:

He stammered, "I ... I ... I wanted to ... um ... I tried to ... well, I really thought I could get it done by this afternoon. I was wrong."

And here is how an ellipsis would show a thought that trails off:

"I tried and tried to convince him, but I couldn't. Oh, well ... "

Fortunately, you'll find that many of today's word-processing programs automatically create a properly spaced ellipsis when you enter three successive periods.

✓ **Killer Tip:** Some of my clients follow style guides that suggest creating an ellipsis with three dots that have a space in between: (. . .) I've found this tricky to work with, because if the first or second dot falls at the end of a line of type, what remains jumps to the next line.

46

Exclamation Points Are Exciting!

Wow!!! Have you noticed how exclamation points sometimes are overused?!! It's over the top!!!!

If you're an enthusiastic person writing about a topic that excites you, it's easy to overdo exclamation points.

Most style guides suggest limiting their use to express a high degree of surprise, incredulity or other strong emotion. Too many exclamation points can leave a reader breathless.

An exclamation point can appear either inside or outside of quotation marks, depending on whether it is part of the quoted material:
- ▶ "How excited you must be about the new baby!" she exclaimed.
- ▶ "Look out! There's a car coming!" the mother shouted at her toddler as he headed down the driveway on his tricycle.

Notice that neither example includes additional punctuation. In other words, there is no comma or period after the closing quotation mark.

These exclamation points are not part of the quoted material:

▶ Please, please don't make me sit through every campaign "debate"!

▶ No, she did *not* call him a "bloviating bag of wind"!

✓ **Killer Tip:** Exclamation points serve a purpose, but using too many is like the little boy who cried wolf: When they appear too frequently, they lose their impact and effectiveness.

47

Hyphens Join and Clarify

Hyphens are joiners. Their use can be more a matter
of taste or writing style than a grammatical absolute.

However, sometimes hyphens are required; they help
to avoid confusion or misunderstanding.

Consider this example:
　The small business seminar begins at 9 a.m.

Is it a small seminar in terms of number of participants,
or is it a seminar for owners of small businesses?

A hyphen adds clarity:
　The small-business seminar begins at 9 a.m.

Adding a hyphen helps you know the seminar will
focus on information helpful to small businesses. The
compound modifier *small-business* further describes the
noun, *seminar.*

**Here are other examples where a hyphen joins two
words that are modifiers, clarifying their meaning:**

- The company's *first-quarter* profits soared.
- Is she seeking a *full-time* job?
- Despite his great wealth, he was a *little-known* man.
- I'm not interested in watching that *second-rate* movie.
- The housing development will soon be ready for *low-income* buyers.

When a modifier that is hyphenated before a noun follows the noun, it often is not hyphenated:

- Company profits for the *first quarter* soared.
- The job became *full time*, which pleased her.
- As a buyer with a *low income*, he qualified for the new housing development.

There are two exceptions to the hyphen guideline:

1. When a compound modifier follows a form of the verb to be (*is, was, were, has been, etc.*), it usually retains the hyphen:

- The man who appeared on the news broadcast *was* little-known.
- We both saw the movie, and we agree with you that it *is* second-rate.

2. When an adverb ends in *ly*, no hyphen is needed, as confusion is unlikely:

- The *barely eaten* chocolate cake sat on the counter for days.
- A *smartly dressed* women entered the elevator.
- Tonight's *hotly contested* title game ended at 10 o'clock.

✓ **Killer Tip:** Hyphens sometimes create multiple-word modifiers: down-on-his-luck drummer, punch-to-the-heart news, already-paid-for tickets, ne'er-do-well cousin, out-of-the-blue suggestion, over-the-top performance.

48

Anti, Multi, Non:
Most Prefixes Don't Require a Hyphen

A prefix is something at the beginning of a word that modifies or changes its meaning.

It usually is not necessary to place a hyphen between the prefix and the word that follows, especially if it begins with a consonant (all letters except vowels a, e, i, o, u):
- ▶ antibody, antifreeze, antisocial
- ▶ noncompliant, nonprofit, nonsectarian
- ▶ postimpressionism, postoperative, postscript

Except for cooperate and coordinate, use a hyphen if the prefix ends with, and the word that follows the prefix starts with, the same vowel:
- ▶ anti-inflammatory
- ▶ pre-eminent
- ▶ ultra-aromatic

Note: Some dictionaries and style guides no longer indicate hyphen use with duplicate letters.

Use a hyphen if the word that follows the prefix is capitalized:
- anti-American
- pre-Christianity
- pro-Darwinism

Use a hyphen if a prefix could be misinterpreted or is not really a prefix:
- **resent**

  I *resent* your invoice

  (I am angry about what you charged me.)
- **re-sent**

  I *re-sent* your invoice.

  (Your invoice didn't reach you, so I sent a copy.)

- **recreate**

  The students *recreate* by playing Dodgeball during recess.
- **re-create**

  We tried to *re-create* a sense of ancient Rome for our school play.

- **resign**

  She resigned from her job with just a week's notice.
- **re-sign**

  She had to re-sign her termination papers because of the date change.

- ✓ **Killer Tip:** You'll find a more complete list of words with suffixes in the appendix. Note how few are hyphenated.

49

Suspended Hyphen Creates Shortcut

We established in Chapter 47 that hyphens are joiners.
They create compound words such as editor-in-chief or
mother-in-law.

Hyphens also create compound modifiers by joining two
or more words that describe something: full-time job,
over-the-counter medication.

When you use a hyphen to create modifiers with the same
base word, you can take a shortcut by using a *suspended
hyphen* to avoid repeating a word.

**Notice that each of these hyphenated examples has
a common base word:**
- ► The program was designed for fifth-*graders* and
  sixth-*graders*.
- ► We need to make both long-*term* and short-*term* plans.
- ► Expect a three-*hour* or four-*hour* delay in my arrival.

**Using a *suspended hyphen* enables you to take
a shortcut and use the base word just once:**
- ► The program was designed for fifth- and sixth-graders.
- ► We need to make both long- and short-term plans.
- ► Expect a three- or four-hour delay in my arrival.

You also can use a suspended hyphen when the base word comes first:

▶ Many small businesses are family-owned and family-financed.

▶ Students undertook *self*-designed and *self*-executed projects.

Here's the shortcut:

▶ Many small businesses are family-owned and -financed.

▶ Students undertook self-designed and -executed projects.

✓ **Killer Tip:** Hyphens have many applications, and guidelines for their use can vary. In general, when a hyphen helps avoid confusion or misunderstanding — or enables you to express something in fewer words — use it.

50

Interrobang:
Punctuation With an Emotional Punch

When you want to express query combined with either outrage or extreme surprise or excitement, both the question mark and the exclamation point let you down.

Combining a question mark with an exclamation point yields the interrobang, a form of punctuation that has been around since 1962. It expresses two emotions but has yet to really catch on.

The Economist, of all publications, featured an article about the interrobang in October 2014, noting that a mere question mark does not always suffice. The writer explained that interrobang inventor Martin K. Speckter, a journalist who went into advertising, expressed a question combined with excitement this way:

What?! A Refrigerator That Makes Its Own Ice Cubes?!

What else but the interrobang fully expresses the emotion of these statements:

▶ Can you believe she replied, "No, I'm not a Badgers fan"‽

▶ Are you saying that Taylor Swift will be performing here in June‽

▶ She shouted, "Can't you tell I'm angry‽"

▶ "What did you expect me to do‽" she screeched.

Note that the interrobang is placed *outside* of the quotation marks in the first example, as it goes with the query that precedes the quoted statement.

The interrobang goes *inside* the quotation marks in the third and last examples, as it goes with the quoted statement.

Interrobangs and other such oddities are special gifts to those of us who love all things grammatical.

✓ **Killer Tip:** Caution: Spellcheck not only considers *interrobang* a misspelling; it instructs you to replace the symbol with a question mark.

51

Parentheses Interrupt Readers
So Use Sparingly

If you need to include incidental information for clarity in your report, your story, your blog or your email, one option is to put it in parentheses.

When the information you enclose in parentheses is not a complete sentence — when it lacks a subject and/or a verb — don't capitalize or use a period:

She had planned to present her report (the summary of her visit to our Ohio subsidiary) at the annual meeting, but she couldn't get the details pulled together in time.

If information is expressed as a complete sentence, the reference could appear in parentheses either within the original sentence or following it:

She had planned to present her travel report at the meeting (She visited our Ohio subsidiary in November.), but she couldn't get the details pulled together in time.

She had planned to present her travel report at the meeting, but she couldn't get the details pulled together in time. (She visited our Ohio subsidiary in November.)

Note in the first of these two examples that if a comma is needed, it generally follows the parenthetical information.

As is so often the case with English, there can be exceptions. Here are two explanations that serve as their own examples:

When you add a remark or an aside — almost as though you are saying something either under your breath or not directly related to the discussion — don't capitalize it. However, do (and please don't argue!) include the punctuation within the parentheses.

When you place a complete sentence in parentheses and it depends on the surrounding material for its meaning (this is one example), do not capitalize the first word or end it with period.

✓ **Killer Tip:** Parentheses can be jarring to readers. Avoid them when you can. When you can't, follow these guidelines. And by the way, parenthe*ses* refers to a pair of marks, an opening and a closing parenthe*sis*.

52

The Period: The Ultimate Insider

Unlike the colon, semicolon, question and exclamation marks, the period *always* goes inside quotation marks. This is one punctuation rule that has no exceptions in American English. (For some Canadian provinces and across the pond, it's a different story.)

He said, "I completed the project last night."

When there is a quote within a quote, the period stays inside both the single and the double quotation marks:

"I was surprised when he said to me, 'I completed the project last night.'"

The period is placed inside quotation marks even with something quoted in part or when a single word is quoted:

▶ He said he was "disappointed and outraged by the incident."
▶ I didn't know what he meant when he claimed to be "outraged."

In general, most two-letter abbreviations have periods:
- ▶ U.N. (United Nations)
- ▶ U.K. (United Kingdom)
- ▶ U.S. (United States)

There can be exceptions. One of those is The Associated Press, for which AP is a registered trademark.

Most three-, four- and five-letter abbreviations do not have periods:
- ▶ Institutions or companies: MIT, IBM, USA, NBC, USAF, YMCA, NASDAQ
- ▶ Common measurements: mph, mpg, rpm,
- ▶ Business titles: CEO, CFO, COO

(See Chapter 27 for more abbreviations and acronyms without periods.)

When using periods with initials that represent names, follow the general guideline of periods with two-letter initials and no period with three-letter initials:
- ▶ J.K. Rowling, T.S. Eliot, A.A. Milne, J.D. Salinger, H.G. Wells, E.E. Cummings
- ▶ JFK, LBJ, MLK, FDR

- ✓ **Killer Tip:** If you put a space between initials in J.K. Rowling or T.S. Eliot, you risk an unnatural separation if the J. or T. fall at the end of a line of type.

53

The Question Mark: Inside or Out?

Commas and periods always go inside quotation marks. The question mark, however, can go inside or outside, depending on whether the quoted material forms a question.

In this example, the quoted material is a question:

Ava asked, "Why didn't Chad wash the windows?"

In this example, the quoted material is not a question:

Did I hear Chad tell Ava, "I washed the windows, but it rained the next day"?

Here are other examples:
▶ Do you think it's OK that the interviewer asked, "Do you plan to get married?"
▶ Who thinks "Do you plan to get married?" is a valid interview question?
▶ I don't consider "What are your marriage plans?" a valid interview question.

Note that in the second and third preceding examples, there is no comma before the question within quotation marks because those words are not attributed to a particular person. The same is true for the second example below.

Nor are there periods within the quotation marks in these second and fourth examples.

▶ Do you remember who said, "All we have to fear is fear itself"?
▶ Does "All you have to fear is fear itself" mean anything to you?
▶ I asked her, "Are you going to the concert?"
▶ Can you believe she told me, "Yes, I've had tickets for three months"?

✓ **Killer Tip:** To ask a question that adds emphasis to each element, consider multiple question marks: What if my luggage is lost? Will I have to buy new clothes? New shoes? Replace my cosmetics?

54

When is a Question Not a Question?

There are times when a sentence appears to be a question, but it really is a polite request that does not require a question mark:

▶ May I ask you to please return my call before 5 o'clock.

▶ Will everyone without a ticket please contact the box office by Friday noon.

▶ Could you please send me a list of your core competencies.

Consider how it would sound if you were to speak these requests. You're not really asking someone to do something to which they could reply yes or no; you're making a request that you expect to be met. In that scenario, you would not raise your pitch at the end.

As indirect questions, these examples don't require a question mark. Contrast them with the true question that follows each:

▶ I wonder if she left her purse in the grocery cart.

▶ Did she leave her purse in the grocery cart?

- ▶ How about leaving 20 minutes early so I can stop at the pharmacy.
- ▶ Could we leave 20 minutes early so I can stop at the pharmacy?

Microsoft Word's spellcheck wants to end each of the first two following statements with a question mark, yet each could be a declaration. Say them without raising your voice at the end:

- ▶ She did a great job, didn't she.
- ▶ Aren't you the clever one.

Now contrast how the pitch of your voice changes with each of these true questions:

- ▶ Did she do a great job?
- ▶ Are you the clever one?

- ✓ **Killer Tip:** When you're writing something that, if spoken, would sound more like a statement than a question — in other words, if you would not be inclined to raise your pitch at the end — don't close with a question mark, regardless of what spellcheck suggests.

55

Italics vs. Quotation Marks for Books, Articles, Music, Plays, Websites

Before computers, we used quotation marks or underlining — either handwritten or created on a typewriter — to identify book titles:

> "Harry Potter and the Deathly Hallows"
> <u>The Hunger Games</u>
> "To Kill a Mockingbird"

Underlining seems ancient today, and although some sources still say to put most titles in quotation marks, I prefer the cleaner, clutter-free look of italics.

So how do you punctuate movie and opera titles, CDs and works of art, radio and television programs, and titles of lectures, speeches, poems and websites? Covering every possibility would take a lot of time and space. Here, in brief, are general guidelines:

Use italics for these categories, considered major works, unless you have other editorial guidelines:

- John Steinbeck's *Of Mice and Men* has been a novel, a play and a movie.
- *The Godfather* is ranked as one the greatest movies ever.
- According to poets.org, Robert Frost's *The Road Less Traveled* is one of the most popular poems of all time.

Reference books are an exception:

The Bible and books used for reference — almanacs, directories, handbooks, dictionaries (Webster's New World College Dictionary) — and software titles (Microsoft Word) don't need quotation marks or italics.

Use quotation marks for smaller works: a short story, a newspaper or magazine article, a chapter, an episode of a TV series:

- Famed author Jack London's "A Piece of Steak" is considered a classic short story.
- "Smile Intensity in Photographs Predicts Longevity" was published in *Psychological Science* in 2010.
- I missed *Madam Secretary* last week, so I'll watch "On the Clock" online before next week's show.
- You'll find "When Does *But* Need A Comma?" on the popular grammar website www.RuthlessEditor.com. (Note: quotation marks for blog title, not for URL)

Use capital letters but not italics or quotation marks for monuments:

- Have you been to Italy to see Michelangelo's *David?*
- Thousands visited The Statue of Liberty today.

✓ **Killer Tip:** Because there are no written-in-stone rules, create your own style guide and follow it consistently. However, keep in mind that style might change from one project to another, depending on your client, employer or reading audience.

56

Semicolons Join, Separate, Clarify

The semicolon is a joiner; it connects two closely related thoughts or statements.

These two elements signal that a semicolon works:
▶ The statement that follows the semicolon relies on the one that precedes it for its meaning.
▶ Statements preceding and following the semicolon could stand alone as complete sentences (each has a subject and a verb).

Here are correct and incorrect examples of semicolons as joiners.
right: Sasha is a gifted gardener; she grows the most beautiful roses.
wrong: Sasha is a gifted gardener; with the most beautiful roses.

right: Use care when washing clothes in hot water; garments can shrink or fade.
wrong: Use care when washing clothes in hot water; as they can shrink or fade.

Note in each wrong example that the phrase following the semicolon could not stand alone as a complete sentence.

In this example, semicolons indicate a clearer separation than commas can accomplish.

> This week's guests are Sen. Jack Jones of Helena, Montana, head of the finance committee; Rep. Sue Smith of Irvine, California, chair of the annual convention; and Gov. Tom Brown of Boston, Massachusetts, leader of the first day's workshop.

Semicolons clarify when commas don't do the job.
Consider the first example below that has only commas, and then consider the second example that uses semicolons:

▶ During the short interval of a week, a house came on the market in my old neighborhood in Austin, Texas, I made an offer that the owner, who'd moved overseas, accepted, and I secured financing at a bank in Madison, Wisconsin, in time to close by the end of the month.

▶ During the short interval of a week, a house came on the market in my old neighborhood in Austin, Texas; I made an offer that the owner, who'd moved overseas, accepted; and I secured financing at a bank in Madison, Wisconsin, in time to close by the end of the month.

Would breaking the example into three distinct sentences be an option? Yes, but using semicolons keeps the flow of the action more connected, underscoring that a number of life-changing events occurred in a short time.

✓ **Killer Tip:** A comma signals a slight pause, a semicolon signals a moderate pause, and a period signals a complete stop.

57

Dump the Double Space!

Original typewriter keys were arranged alphabetically. As users gained speed, they found that keys struck most often were right next to each other, causing frequent jams. At least that's what so-called historical accounts claim.

Typewriter inventor Christopher Latham Sholes rearranged the keys in 1873 to what became known as the QWERTY keyboard (top row of letters, the first six left to right). We since have learned that telegraph operators, with their need to quickly transcribe messages, were more influential in providing input about what might work better than Sholes' original alphabetical key arrangement.

Today's computer keyboards and their tablet and smart-phone counterparts still mimic their forerunner, the typewriter. But font selections have grown exponentially.

Monospaced vs. Proportional Fonts

Today's Courier harkens back to typewriter days and *monospaced* fonts; each letter, whether a lowercase i or a lowercase m, has a fixed width and takes up equal space when it makes an impression on paper or on a screen. If you learned keystrokes on a typewriter, you might be among those who create two spaces after a period, which was necessary to clearly mark the end of a sentence created with monospaced fonts.

But if you still press your spacebar twice at the end of a sentence, whether on an iPad, smartphone or laptop, you risk appearing out-of-date, resistant to change — or maybe even a bit unprofessional. Today's proportional font spacing makes two spaces unnecessary.

Compare Courier and Lucida with Times and Arial
Consider the following four fonts. Courier and Lucida are *monotype* fonts. Times and Arial are *proportional* fonts. Your device automatically creates appropriate between-letter spacing with *proportional* fonts for ease of reading and to conserve space.

This is 10-point Courier. See the difference?

This is 10-point Lucida. See the difference?

This is 10-point Times. See the difference?

This is 10-point Arial. See the difference?

Pick up any magazine, book or newspaper. Is there a significant space after each period? Or is there minimal white space, just enough to let you know that one sentence is ending and the next is beginning?

And, yes, this single-space guideline also applies to spacing after colons and semicolons, and to sentences that end with question marks and exclamation points.

✓ **Killer Tip:** If you're still a double-spacer, don't be an old dog who can't learn new tricks; be a contemporary keyboarder.

3 BONUS TIPS

The biggest problem with communication
is the illusion that it has been accomplished.

— Carl Sandburg

Tips For Better Emails

Email reigns as the communication mode of choice in the business world. Billions of work-related emails are sent and received every day.

Make sure your first email to a potential client creates a positive first impression. You might not get a second chance.

Because emails lack facial expression, tone of voice and body language, carelessly composed messages can create misunderstandings, harm customer relationships, erode loyalty and lose business.

Brushing up on grammar is a good first step to improving how you communicate electronically. Here are a dozen other tips to help you fine-tune your email skills.

Twelve Tips for Better Emails:
1. Leave the TO field blank until you are ready to press SEND.
2. Use the SUBJECT line to inform rather than just identify; it should read like a headline that briefly summarizes your message and draws in the reader.
3. Base your message content on your recipient's need to know. Consider journalism's 5 W's: Who, What, When, Where, Why (and sometimes How).
4. Use standard grammar and spelling.

5. Use short words, short sentences (8–12 words), and short paragraphs (50 words or fewer = 3 or 4 sentences) with a line space between paragraphs.
6. Use bullet points and numbers to organize information.
7. Fill no more than one laptop computer screen.
8. Keep your spellcheck function on at all times, and reread your message before sending.
9. If an attachment is necessary, add it before you start to compose your email. We've all received or sent emails that refer to missing attachments.
10. Reply the same business day, even if it's just to confirm receipt and advise the sender when you will respond in full.
11. Respond to all questions posed, and try to anticipate others to reduce the number of back-and-forth messages.
12. If the topic changes in an ongoing thread, start a new email with its own thread.

✓ **Killer Tip:** Follow my Ruthless Editor's guide to the Three C's of Effective Writing — Clear, Concise, grammatically Correct — in every type of communication, including email. You'll save yourself and your recipients time and aggravation, and you'll save your organization money.

The Power of Thank You

*The deepest principle in human nature
is the craving to be appreciated.*
— William James

How often do you take time to show appreciation?

I remember writing a profile of a woman who was retiring from a career in banking. When I interviewed her, she said that one of the most pleasant aspects of her job was the knowledge that she truly was helping people.

She added that she especially appreciated "the terrific customers whose moms taught them how to say thank you. I love helping, but I also love to hear 'Thank you.'"

The following weekend I conducted a training session that included material on business etiquette. Because handwritten thank-you notes are so rare, I encourage people to send them. It not only makes the recipient feel good; it sets you apart and makes you memorable — a good thing in our competitive business world.

I asked the group of 20 if any had received a handwritten thank-you note in the last month. One woman raised her hand and reported that of 100 people who attended an event she had planned and executed, she received one written thank-you.

It takes very little energy and time to speak words of appreciation, and you need only three or four lines for a written thank-you message:

▶ Mention the occasion or the event.
▶ Say why it was important / special / appreciated.
▶ Express thanks for the time and effort that went into hosting it.

Hello, Jennifer,

What a lovely business open house you held Tuesday evening. Your team did a magnificent job of decorating your lobby. It was so nice to meet and greet friends, colleagues and coworkers in an informal setting

Thanks for the time and energy you and your staff spent planning and hosting this special gathering.

Sincerely,

Kathleen Watson

Find a few minutes every day to show appreciation to the people who make your job or your life easier or more pleasant.

✓ **Killer Quote:** "Cultivate the habit of being grateful for every good thing that comes to you, and to give thanks continuously." — Ralph Waldo Emerson

No Problem? No Thanks.

*Kind words can be short and easy to speak,
but their echoes are truly endless.*
— Mother Teresa

I encourage people to speak — and write — words of thanks, in both our personal and business lives. We all like to know our efforts are recognized and appreciated.

But what about accepting thanks? Do you do it graciously?

"No problem" so often is uttered in reply to a spoken expression of thanks.

I despair at the lack of civility and graciousness in much of today's public discourse. The utterance "no problem" is anything but gracious.

In fact, consider that it is shorthand for "It was not a problem for me to help you."

Then consider whether it ever should be a problem or imposition for us to render help to someone.

"No problem" is an even more inappropriate response when the help for which you have thanked someone is a service you in essence are paying for: a cashier handing you change and a receipt; a bagger at the supermarket handing you your tote of groceries; a flight attendant pouring you a cup of coffee.

Add to that the negative connotations of "no" and "problem," and it's easy to see why these responses are better:

► You're welcome.
► My pleasure.
► I was happy to do it.
► I'm glad I could help.

Let's be positive and gracious when acknowledging someone's expression of thanks. It might serve as a small step in elevating the tone of our discourse in general.

APPENDIX

Parts of Speech

It's hard to talk about grammar without understanding the basic parts of speech. Many grammarians recognize eight key categories: **noun, verb, adjective, adverb, pronoun, conjunction, preposition, interjection**.

The following list includes select other categories covered in this book: **proper noun, collective noun, possessive pronoun, indefinite pronoun, gerund, object, complete sentence, compound sentence**.

Noun
a person, place or thing
girl | downtown | car

Proper Noun
specific people, places or things; capitalize them
Sarah | The Loop | Ford Fusion

Collective Noun
a group of people or things
team | committee | flock

Pronoun
used in place of a noun
she | him | they | who | it

Possessive Pronoun
indicates ownership
my, mine | your, yours
her, hers | his | its | ours | their

Indefinite Pronoun
refers to nonspecific persons or things
all | another | any | anybody
nobody | several | some

Verb

shows action; can include being or having something
The girl *runs*. She *is* smart and *has* brown hair.

Gerund

an *–ing* form of a verb that is used as a noun
Walking is good exercise. My *yelling* upset him.

Adjective

describes or tells you more about a noun
The *tall* girl was late for school. The *historic* church is
on the corner.

Adverb

gives extra information about verbs; tells how, when
or where things happen; often ends in *ly*
The girl walked *quickly* to the entrance. Her teacher
immediately greeted her.

Object

receiver of action
He kicked the *ball*. She slung her *tote* over her shoulder.

Complete (or simple) Sentence

has subject and verb and just one thing to say
She placed the order today. It will arrive on Tuesday.

Compound (or complex) Sentence

has more than one thing to say
She placed the order today, and it will arrive on Tuesday.
I would have walked, but it started to rain.

Conjunction

connects words or thoughts
for | and | nor | but | or | yet | so
because | when | while | unless | whether
He wants to visit Paris, Rome *and* Berlin.

The order will ship on Monday, *so* it should arrive on Wednesday.

I told him to go home *whether* he wants to or not.

Preposition
tells where or when things happen
on | in | under | over | before | during | after
She set her books *on* the table *before* she sat down.

Article
considered an adjective because it provides information about a noun
a | an | the

Interjections
words that express emotions
Hey! Oops! Yay! Wow! Yikes!

Standard English
the form of the English language widely accepted as the usual correct form

Most Words With a Prefix Don't Need a Hyphen

***ante:* before**
antebellum
antecedent
anteroom

***anti:* against**
antidepressant
antipollution
antitrust

***bi:* two**
biannual
bilateral
bipolar

***co:* together, jointly**
co-chair
co-owner
co-sponsor

No hyphen in other combinations
coexist
cooperate
copay

***dis:* opposite of**
disassemble
disinterested
disobedience

***extra:* outside of, beyond**
extracurricular
extramarital
extraterrestrial

***infra:* below**
infrastructure
infrared

***inter:* between, among**
interchange
interoffice
internet

***intra:* inside, within**
intracellular
intramural
intranet

***multi:* many, multiple, much**
multicolored
multidimensional
multinational

***non:* not, other than, reverse of**
nonfiction
nonissue
nontraditional

***out / over:* to exceed or surpass**
outlearn
outperform

outproduce
overachieve
overpay
oversensitive

para: **aside from, alongside**
paralegal
paramilitary
parasailing

post: **following, after**
postgraduate
postmodern
postelection

pre: **coming before**
precondition
pre-eminent, pre-exist, pre-empt
pregame
prenatal

re: **again, anew**
repaint
re-evaluate, re-enter, re-examine
reintroduce

semi: **half of**
semicircle
semiconscious
semifinal

sub: **under, below**
subspecialty
subhuman
subtropical

un: **opposite or reverse of**
unconstitutional
undiminished
unwearable

under: **below or beneath**
underestimate
underdeveloped
underachiever

Ruthless Editor's Top 10 Misused Words: Can You Make the Right Choice?

1. **adverse / averse**
   He was not **adverse/averse** to taking the medication, but he had an **adverse/averse** reaction.

2. **affect / effect**
   Today's storm will **affect/effect** air traffic, but it should not have an **affect/effect** on tomorrow's flights.

3. **anxious / eager**
   I'm **anxious/eager** about my performance review, but I'm **anxious/eager** to have it behind me.

4. **bad / badly**
   He felt **bad/badly** that he didn't make the tennis finals, but he played **bad/badly**.

5. **ensure / insure**
   To **ensure/insure** that you can call a doctor when your children are ill, we will **ensure/insure** your entire family.

6. **farther / further**
   The **farther/further** they walked, the **farther/further** engrossed they became in conversation.

7. **fewer / less**
   Fewer/less people signed up for the tournament this year, so I'll need **fewer/less** food than I had planned.

8. **flout / flaunt**
   Despite warnings, students continue to **flout/flaunt** the law when they **flout/flaunt** riding mopeds on the sidewalk.

9. **good / well**
   Although I feel **good/well** in general, I'm not sure I have the strength to perform **good/well** in the recital.

10. **its / it's**
    Its/It's up to you, but I hope you'll leave the key in **its/it's** usual place.   (answers on next page)

Top 10 Misused Words: Answers

1. **averse** (having strong dislike or opposition to), then **adverse** (harmful, unfavorable)
2. **affect** (verb: to change or influence something), then **effect** (noun: result of an action).
3. **anxious** (feeling worry or unease), then **eager** (keen interest or desire)
4. **bad** (adjective; modifies a noun or pronoun), then **badly** (adverb; describes an action)
5. **ensure** (to make certain), then **insure** (to safeguard against loss, usually by securing insurance coverage)
6. **farther** (greater distance), then **further** (to a greater extent)
7. **fewer** (things you can count), then **less** (quantity uncountable in terms of number
8. **flout** (to openly disregard, as a rule, law or accepted practice), then **flaunt** (to display or make a great show of)
9. **good** (adjective; describes a noun or pronoun), then **well** (adverb; describes an action)
10. **it's** (contraction for it is), **its** (possessive of it)

Test Your Knowledge: 12 Confusing Caps

Here are a dozen terms that often are written incorrectly. Some are capitalized and should not be; others should not be capitalized but are. Take the test, and then check the next page to find answers and explanations.

1. band-aid | Band-Aid
2. cellophane | Cellophane
3. crock-pot | Crock-Pot
4. earth | Earth
5. fiberglass | Fiberglas
6. formica | Formica
7. jacuzzi | Jacuzzi
8. jello | Jello
9. kleenex | Kleenex
10. popsicle | Popsicle
11. q-tips | Q-tips
12. realtor | Realtor

(answers on next page)

Twelve Confusing Caps: Answers

1. **Band-Aid** (trademark for an adhesive bandage)
2. **cellophane** (former trademark for thin, clear, moisture-proof wrap; now a generic term)
3. **Crock-Pot** (brand name for a slow cooker)
4. **Earth** when referring to it as a planet (How far is Earth from Mars?) But earth when referring to planet we live on or to the ground or soil (What on earth are you saying? He's down to earth.)
5. **Fiberglas** (trademark for fiberglass; note single *s*)
6. **Formica** (trademark for laminated plastic)
7. **Jacuzzi** (trademark of hot tubs, bathtubs; company also makes mattresses and toilets)
8. **Jell-O** is the trademark; jello is generic for flavored gelatin.
9. **Kleenex** (trademark for brand of facial tissue)
10. **Popsicle** (trademark; other brands use "ice pops" or "freezer pops")
11. **Q-tips** (trademark for a brand of cotton swabs)
12. **Realtor** (member of the National Association of Realtors; real estate agent is preferred generic term) Note: pronounced *Re-al-tor*, not *Real-a-tor*

Check Your Word and Punctuation IQ

Which are correct?

Words
1. Facebook has some concerning content.
   Facebook has some disconcerting content.
2. My boss is taking Jim and I to lunch.
   My boss is taking Jim and me to lunch.
3. If you see someone using the back door, please direct them to the front.
   If you see people using the back door, please direct them to the front.
4. I wish I was on a Florida beach.
   I wish I were on a Florida beach.
5. He's the kind of person that can't take a joke.
   He's the kind of person who can't take a joke.

Punctuation
1. He invited me to join the Mac users group.
   He invited me to join the Mac users' group.
2. We appreciate your support, and we hope you'll help again next year.
   We appreciate your support and we hope you'll help again next year.
3. Last summer I traveled to Austin, Texas, Oberlin, Ohio, Galena, Illinois, and Bend, Oregon.
   Last summer I traveled to Austin, Texas; Oberlin, Ohio; Galena, Illinois; and Bend, Oregon.
4. Will you please send me a list of your core competencies?
   Will you please send me a list of your core competencies.
5. I don't know why he claimed to be "outraged".
   I don't know why he claimed to be "outraged."

(answers on next page)

Words Answers:

1. Facebook has some *disconcerting* content.
   (disconcerting: troubling, disturbing, unsettling)
2. My boss is taking Jim and *me* to lunch. (My boss is taking me … and Jim.)
3. If you see *people* using the back door, please direct *them* to the front. (people, them: both plural)
4. I wish I *were* on a Florida beach. (I'm not there yet.)
5. He's the kind of person *who* can't take a joke. (Who is for people; that is for objects or unfamiliar animals.)

Punctuation Answers:

1. He invited me to join the Mac *users* group. (no apostrophe: descriptive instead of possessive)
2. We appreciate your support, and we hope you'll help again next year. (comma before *and* with two complete sentences)
3. Last summer I traveled to Austin, Texas; Oberlin, Ohio; Galena, Illinois; and Bend, Oregon. (a semi-colon creates a clearer separation than a comma does)
4. Will you please send me a list of your core competencies. (period: is a request, not a question)
5. I didn't know what he meant when he claimed to be "outraged." (period always inside quotation marks)

INDEX

Acknowledgements

I extend gratitude and appreciation to …

Donna Collingwood, without whose urging this book would not exist. My graphic designer, colleague and friend, Donna convinced me the project was doable and got me started with her enthusiasm and concepts for a cover design and page format.

Jim Miller, who serendipitously crossed my path when I was pulling all of the elements together. He was my technical expert, my sharp-eyed and forthright editor, and my encourager-in-chief through the final stages, patiently preparing me for the publication steps.

Dorothy Nuzum, my high school homeroom adviser and senior year English teacher. Mrs. Nuzum taught me the value of rewriting … rewriting … rewriting.

Rae Miller, my undergrad journalism instructor, who saw my potential and helped me fine-tune my skills. I have treasured her instruction and support, and I value her friendship to this day.

Laura Browning, Associated Press expert and sharp-eyed first-stage editor; and Barbara Samuel, seasoned writer, editor, colleague and friend who helped fine-tune the final version.

About the Author

Grammar expert Kathleen Watson, also known as The Ruthless Editor, has nearly three decades of writing and editing experience in both corporate and academic worlds. She has taught business people how to fine-tune their communication style, college students how to strengthen their writing, and Ph.D. candidates how to polish their dissertations. Kathy also has experience as a fiction and nonfiction book copy editor, working with a mix of new and experienced authors. In addition to writing her own book on grammar, she blogs at RuthlessEditor.com, sharing weekly tips on how to write to get the job you want, earn the promotion you've worked hard for, and artfully explain your best ideas. An avid reader who divides her time between Arizona and Wisconsin, she enjoys exploring the contrasts, history and unique scenic wonders of each state.

Address inquires to the author via:
email: Kathy@RuthlessEditor.com
website: www.RuthlessEditor.com

Contact the author for quantity pricing
of 10 or more books.

Made in the USA
Middletown, DE
31 December 2016